Arthur

Arthur

The dog who crossed the jungle to find a home

MIKAEL LINDNORD

with Val Hudson

www.tworoadsbooks.com

First published in Great Britain in 2016 by Two Roads
An imprint of John Murray Press
An Hachette UK company

1

Copyright © Mikael Lindnord 2016

A CIP catalogue record for this title is available from the British Library

Hardback ISBN 978-1-4736-25235
Trade Paperback ISBN 978-1-4736-25242
Ebook ISBN 978-1-4736-25280

636·70832

Typeset in Cochin by Hewer Text UK Ltd, Edinburgh
The picture credits on page 275 constitute an extension of this copyright page
Printed and bound by CPI Group (UK) Ltd, Croydon, CR0 4YY

John Murray Press policy is to use papers that are natural, renewable
and recyclable products and made from wood grown in sustainable
forests. The logging and manufacturing processes are expected to
conform to the environmental regulations of the country of origin.

Two Roads
John Murray Press
Hodder & Stoughton Ltd
Carmelite House
50 Victoria Embankment
London EC4Y 0DZ

MAA

5\16
20/12/16.

WITHDRAWN

'I never set out to have a dog.
But I feel there is something of Arthur in me.
Meeting Arthur and bringing him home is the single best
*   thing I have ever done.'*

Atlantic
Ocean

MOMPICHE Quito

Pacific Ocean

Atlantic
Ocean

N
W   E
S

Contents

Chapter 1

A Sporting Chance

'People who do adventure racing are not normal'

Örnsköldsvik, November 2015

It's eleven thirty at night, and I'm just beginning to hit my stride with the emails that have been piling up in my in-box. We are only days away from setting off for the Adventure Racing World Championship in Brazil – the highlight of the year's racing schedule. There are a hundred things to organise, and my desk is overflowing with lists of things to take, and lists of things to do, before my team and I set off.

Outside there's a wind howling, and it's started to rain, but our upstairs office is warm. Warm and comfortable – and smelling just a little bit of wet dog. My feet aren't remotely cold, but if they were I'd only have to move them a couple of inches and they'd be cosy and safe beneath a familiar furry body.

Arthur.

Half asleep as he lies under the desk, adjusting his front left paw so it's in the perfect, comfortable Arthur-ish position. If I shut my eyes, now or at any time, I can see him in this favourite position. His long body panting gently, his big lion-like head pointing towards me expect-antly, and one of his front paws tucked under him as if he were saving it for later. I don't have to look below the desk to know what he's doing. I can hear from the snuffle and the sigh of contentment that he's making himself comfortable for as long as it takes me to do my work.

Helena and the children are asleep downstairs. It's a rare moment of quiet in a house that's usually full of activ-ity and noise. Two-year-old Philippa is perfect and ador-able and I'd do anything in the world for her, but her thirst for new adventures and new things to play with sometimes means waking up her little brother.

Thor is only three months old, so he can't really be expected to know when it's playtime and when it's sleep time. Mostly he is beautifully behaved – he eats, sleeps, eats, sleeps and that's pretty much it – but he can be a bit noisy too. I guess with two people in the house under three, you have to expect noise and a little bit of mess.

But there's a serene presence in the middle of all this, and as I look down below the desk to check on him, Arthur looks up at me with the trusting expression that I never tire of seeing. I scratch his head, just behind his ear. Most of him is a rich golden colour, but his ears – through the unique mixture of dog genes that makes up Arthur – are a delicate shade of orange. I love these ears, and the way they fly up in the air when he's running fast over the mountains.

But at the moment there's no running; there's just a sleepy contentment. Happy to know that I'm safely in his sight, he puts his big head back down on to his paw and closes his eyes.

As I start to make the final preparations for this year's championships, I can't help gazing at Arthur in a little bit of wonder. This time last year, I had no idea he even

existed. Let alone that he would become a part of me, a part of our family. I started thinking of how extraordinary it is that we are here together, despite all the odds having been so stacked against us . . .

Örnsköldsvik, 1993

'No, not you, Mikael. You're out. Not good enough.'

I stopped in the middle of tying up my hockey boots and looked up at my coach aghast.

'You can stay if you like,' he went on. 'But I won't be letting you play. I suggest you pack your things and say goodbye.'

He turned away from me, walked out of the locker room and moved out to the ice to talk to the rest of the class. He led three of them on to the rink and started directing them in a new training exercise. As he sped off, he looked like he was completely unaware of the hammer blow he'd just dealt me.

It felt like my insides had turned to water. Not. In. The. Team. I was seventeen years old, and being in the ice hockey team was pretty much all I'd ever wanted, all I'd been aiming for and training for these past five years. I hadn't missed a single training session, I'd done everything that had been asked of me. I did my very best, trained off-season and extra on rest days. I put all my energy, everything I had into it.

The words 'not good enough' seemed to echo around the skating arena. I bent down to put my gear back in my bag, not wanting anyone to see the expression on my face. When I'd packed everything away, I looked at my school-mates. I didn't know it then but it would be more than twenty years before I entered that locker room again.

As they went off to start the training session, it seemed to be business as usual for them. Nobody realised that something in Mikael Lindnord had just died a little.

For anyone born and brought up in Örnsköldsvik, northern Sweden, ice hockey was pretty much the holy grail of what you could do. In fact, it was the holy grail wherever you were born in Sweden. Our country is unusual in this respect: you can be mediocre at anything, that's fine, mediocre is fine. But if there's one thing you should really, really excel at it is hockey. That's the sport that more than any other – even soccer, even orienteering and skiing – commands respect.

Ever since I was a small boy I put my heart and soul into sport. I'm not a natural talent, but I have always loved sports and been super-competitive. Years before, when I was only about ten, I was at a volleyball practice at school. It was only a practice, the score didn't really matter as such, yet when the coach called the ball out because he said it had hit the roof, I hit the roof too. I was sure the ball was still in play and I wouldn't accept his call. I must have been infuriating to teach at that age, but I was simply determined to win. Even in a practice session.

I guess the coaches could see the determination, and the effort, but in the end they didn't see enough skill.

I remember going home at the end of that day, wondering how I'd tell my parents that I wasn't in the team. They knew how much it meant to me, and indeed my mother had spent most of the previous twelve years driving me to endless hockey practices and other sports events. I suppose she might have got bored during all those years of waiting in the car for me to finish whatever training session I was at, but if she did she'd never say so. Once, she was the last mother waiting by quite some time. I'd got lost during an orienteering race and was well behind everyone else. And yet that didn't stop me painstakingly making sure that I went to all the checkpoints to get my card stamped. They'd told me to finish the whole course, so finish it I did. Looking back, I realise now that I was never going to be a quitter.

My father was in the military and worked for the United Nations, a job I didn't really understand in those days, and anyway he never really talked about his work. But I knew it was important and time-consuming.

It also meant that he had the option of working abroad for a year. He didn't have to, but he had wanted to. So we – my parents, me aged twelve, my sister aged seven – were uprooted from our lives in Sweden to go and live on the other side of the world. For the first six months we were to live in Damascus. And then for the next six months we were to live in Cairo.

Nowadays I'm glad I had that year abroad, and in such frighteningly unfamiliar places. Like a lot of not-always-pleasant experiences that one has in life, I can look back on it and realise that actually I learned things, things that made me understand the world a little bit better.

At the time it didn't feel like it, though. And when it came to learning things at school, I actually learned precious little. I had to go to the Pakistani school in Damascus, where the teachers were brutal. All our lessons were in English, which I didn't speak well then. Maths was my weakest subject (in fact, I was pretty average at most sciences and things that involved numbers), so imagine how hard an average Swedish boy found it to be taught maths in English. Sometimes we were told to learn our times tables overnight, and when I couldn't say them the next day, which I hardly ever could, I'd be beaten. My mother would help me with my homework, but even so, in class I'd get question after question wrong, and nearly every time I got my ears pulled for being stupid. Pulled hard – with a firm grip and a forward motion. I'm amazed I don't have enormous ears, or they don't point forward in an unusual way.

It was a very hard time. Not only was I being beaten, but I was desperately homesick for Sweden. I really, really missed the place and all my friends. But eventually my father went to the school and told the principals – two rather terrifying women – that it wasn't acceptable to beat a Swedish citizen like this, even a small one. After that, the beating stopped, but I was so tired at the end of the day and I still had to stay up doing homework until it was time for bed. It was constant punishment, and it isn't how school should be. The memory still haunts me, even thirty years later.

But those six months, and the six months in Cairo, did teach me something about how other people live with each other, or how they *should* live with each other. Just watching people from different cultures having to get used to being with each other was a lesson in itself. And because I'd had such a hard time learning in another language, I think I'll always have sympathy for people who come to a strange country and are suddenly expected to be able to do everything in a strange language.

Shortly after we got back to Sweden, we moved to Örnsköldsvik, the same town where we still live today. It's a great part of the world, where you can ski, trek, bike, swim, play sport – all within a few minutes of home.

The city is in the heart of a beautiful archipelago and the area known as the High Coast – the Höga Kusten. The combination of steep hills, small islands and forests makes for fantastic country – it looks beautiful at any time of the year, and the trails are some of the most spectacular anywhere in the world.

When I was growing up, if I wasn't playing ice hockey I'd be biking or skiing – we had great skiing holidays as children – or skating. I liked skating, even though I had a bit of a problem with it for many years. I had a pair of skates that didn't fit properly. Every time I put them on I had so much pain. I'd look around me at everyone else, and they didn't seem to be troubled by their skates. I thought everyone must be in pain like me, and I couldn't understand why they weren't showing it. It was only years later, when I had skates that fitted, that I realised what a difference it made – and in fact now, at thirty-nine, I am a better skater than I was when I was younger and training five or six hours a week. I'd also play soccer during the summer – just for fun; with this sport I did know I didn't have the skill to really succeed.

And then that summer, the summer I didn't make it to the hockey team, I discovered something that took the edge off my disappointment. A girl called Helena.

It was the summer of 1993, the exams were over and we were free to be outside and to have late nights, and even the odd secret drink when our parents weren't look-ing. I had been going out with a girl at high school since I was fifteen, so she and I had been together for nearly three years. Like most of my friends, I thought of myself as quite the grown-up, but looking back on the seven-teen-going-on-eighteen-year-old me, I guess I wasn't really that sophisticated after all. Having a girlfriend and playing lots of sport didn't necessarily make you mature.

A group of us decided to celebrate the beginning of the holidays by going to a dance in the centre of town. We knew people from at least two other schools would be there, so we all thought – especially those friends who were single – there'd be new boys and girls there. And that could only be a good thing.

It was noisy and dark, as these places so often are, but I immediately noticed a glint of golden hair at the other side of the room. As I edged closer I could see this awesomely lovely girl. She looked bright and fun, and gorgeous. We talked a bit – or as much as you could talk with all the noise – but then we said goodnight. I'd been able to establish that she was younger than me, sixteen, and she loved sport, especially horse riding. Also that she wasn't with anyone. But I was, so I had to go.

Somehow, though, I knew in my heart that this was the real thing, and I knew I had to break up with my girl-friend before I could do anything about it. Once that hard part was over, the next difficult bit was to pursue Helena. The first time I asked to go round and see her, she said I couldn't as she was just off to a week's riding camp.

But I didn't let that put me off. I could see how impor-tant her riding was to her, and that this wasn't just some excuse. Also I could see that she was a little bit nervous, which made me even more sure that she did want to see me. Gradually we got to know each other, and saw more and more of each other. In between her riding and my hockey, of course.

She said later that she could tell straight away that I was 'a very special guy'. I don't know about that, but I do know it's wonderful that all these years later she still thinks I'm a special guy.

If having met the love of your life is a very grown-up experience, then so too is military service. When I was eighteen, military service was compulsory, though since 2010 you only get to do military exercises if you're going into the army professionally. But I do think there's an argument for making military service compulsory still. It gives you a discipline and a structure, and it makes you find things out about yourself. For me, it was the beginning of the rest of my life.

I elected to do fifteen months of military training, the maximum, although after what had happened with the ice hockey team I felt desperately insecure – terrified even – as to whether or not I'd make it. But I was determined to do whatever it would take to succeed.

Throughout my childhood I was told that I was weak. I knew my father's expectations of me weren't high; I remember as if it were yesterday him telling me that he didn't think I could make it. Maybe this was because, being in the military himself, he had seen so many boys like me broken by the tough, hard work that you had to do. And maybe his idea that I was 'weak' was something to do with my hatred of confrontation – which I do hate; I feel really bad after any confrontation for a long time afterwards. But actually weak? Rather, I felt I had something to prove, not just to myself but to him and everyone else.

After the first tests of physical fitness and endurance, I began to think that maybe I was right and my father was wrong. This was where I belonged.

For one of the early tests, fifty-five of us set off on a hugely gruelling march over the mountains of Kiruna, the biggest, northernmost town in Sweden, not far from the Finnish border, with fifty-kilo backpacks, and only our own resources to make it to the end. As the march got tougher and tougher people dropped out. Not many were expected to see it through to the end of the march, and of the fifty-five – all judged to be physically very fit – only twenty-two went on to become Green Beret Rangers.

I was so happy to have proved that I had the kind of toughness that it took to win through. I felt it was one in the eye to the officers who had yelled and shouted insults at me in the past.

When it came to my turn to lead the boys, I thought I should give them a taste of the medicine that I had suffered. On a day I shall never forget, I stood in front of them to give them my great speech. I think I believed then that the louder I shouted, the more I bullied, the tougher I would seem and the more the men would admire me. I think I must have thought that the more noise I made the less likely my basic insecurities would be found out.

It did not go well. I went red in the face, I forgot some of the words I wanted to say and my voice cracked in the middle of my shouts. But despite this failure of public speaking, I still felt that I had what it takes to succeed in the military.

From there, we went on to do months of even more demanding exercises – I guess we were being trained to be warriors, to survive, to kill rather than be killed. We'd do most of our exercises as if on a defence mission around the Russian border. Every day was different – we might be chased by dogs, or by other bands of soldiers. Often we ran out of food, and had to sneak up on imaginary enemy lines under fire. And rather like in the movies of that time, always the 'enemy' was from the east.

As the weeks progressed I discovered that I was right – I was strong. Not just physically strong, but strong in my head. Willpower strong. We would be carrying two guys, racing and still winning. I could keep going when everyone around me had given up; I found I had huge reserves of stamina, plus an ability to go without sleep that seemed to be above and beyond anyone else's.

And along with all this I discovered something else, something that would change my life. I discovered that I had what translates from Swedish as 'troopscharm': the ability to take guys with me. Not just by telling them what to do, but also by showing them what to do. I learned to lead by example. I didn't shout or insult, I was just positive. I was a natural leader.

On one exercise we were all out in the bush and it got incredibly cold. Numbingly, buttock-clenchingly, toe-freezingly cold. We could see our breath, we could see our eyelashes freeze even as we blinked.

Some people were finding it almost too tough, but I found that not only did I not have a problem with the cold and the exhaustion, but that I could also show them that it was OK, we could get through. If we helped each other and kept going, we'd make it together. One or two guys had to be carried, another had to be joked into carrying on up the last mountain when he'd almost given up. Somehow or other I got us all to the end of the exercise, in good spirits and all, thankfully, alive.

Then, after one particularly tough test out in the mountains – where a troop of thirty of us crossed difficult terrain in freezing temperatures for ten days at a stretch – we got back to base to be told that there would be a test the following morning against the rest of the regiment. We were all sore, sick and exhausted. It was beyond belief that we were expected to perform to peak standards at dawn the following morning. Of the thirty of us, twenty-six found a reason or a doctor's note not to do the test.

Although a part of me thought they were just seeing if we'd even turn up, I got up at dawn and presented myself for duty. It was for real. It was a serious race, and there was no going back. So we did the competition, sprinted like maniacs and came in only just behind the winners – and top overall.

We crossed the finish line and were bending over, utterly exhausted, breathless but slightly exhilarated at what we had achieved. Our commanding officer came over to us. 'OK guys. Good job. You are now the new Number One Platoon Ranger Officers.'

As I saluted him, sweat pouring down my face, I felt a thrill of pride and satisfaction that I can still feel to this day. This was the first time I had been told I was the best. And it was a moment to savour.

All sorts of things followed from that – where I used to blush and hate talking to large groups of people, now I was confident at public speaking; where before I would take a back seat, now I would take command and show the way. But mostly I realised that I could succeed, that I was someone who could lead, see the big picture, have confidence – and have the maturity to know all that.

I was growing up.

Chapter 2

Finding the Way

*'You can't get to where you want to go if
you don't know where you are'*

Örnsköldsvik, 2015

The sun's starting to break through in the first moments
of dawn, and I've just run up to the top of my favourite
mountain. It's still autumn, so there's no sign of snow yet,
and you can see the naked wooden ski jump looming
rather terrifyingly out of the gloom.

I can feel the familiar gasping pain as I lean over to recover my breath. I've parked the car at the top, so that I can run down and up again and finish at the highest point. I look back down the trail, expecting to see a familiar golden shape. Hmm. No sign of Arthur.

I decide not to panic. Even though the forests and mountains of Sweden are so different to the jungles of Ecuador where Arthur spent his first mysterious years, he has a way of orienteering himself.

It mostly involves going back to the point where he's last seen me, or where I've parked the car. But it is getting late, and I start to feel a hard knot of worry in my stomach. I set off at great speed down the mountain, bouncing in between the rocks and roots. I am well used to this kind of running, so it is not long before I am halfway down the trail.

Still no sign of Arthur. I think back to how lost we were together the day after we first met, me and my team misreading the map, Arthur unwittingly leading us even further astray. Perhaps Arthur's internal compass has let him down this morning . . .

The knot in my stomach seems to grow tighter, and I turn round to go back to the top. We are way too far away from home for Arthur to make his way there by himself, so he must be somewhere near. But it's getting later and later, and running uphill is slower work than coming down.

As I reach the top of the hill and see the outline of the ski jump against the still-grey sky, I head round the back towards the car. Nothing there but a few loose rocks.

Then suddenly there's a woof. From behind the car comes a golden bundle of fur and paws and barking. Arthur bounds towards me as if he hasn't seen me for months. He jumps up at me, higher and higher, barking in an 'isn't this fun?' kind of way. I am so happy to see him that I don't mind that he's being a bit rough and practically knocking me off my feet. I kneel down and put my face next to his and my arms round his furry body.

Not lost after all.

To Åre and Beyond, 1995 Onwards

Of all the things I hate, getting lost is right up near the top of the list. Maybe it's the memory of all those hours spent trying to find the checkpoints in the forest when I was a boy. Maybe it's the feeling of rising panic I still get when I look at a muddied map in the middle of the jungle and have NO IDEA which path we're on. Or maybe it's just that getting lost is always the first step to losing. But whatever causes it, I hate that feeling of helplessness.

Happily, my spell in the military did a lot to make me more confident about navigation. There's nothing like having thirty guys dependent on you getting the map coordinates right in a temperature of minus-35 to focus the mind.

I was beginning to realise there were things I was good at, and my favourite thing I was good at was skiing. We did plenty of cross-country skiing in the military; I knew I was getting better and better at it and I found I couldn't get enough of it. I often spent my leave going mountain-skiing with other cadets. The army had a cabin in the small ski resort of Riksgränsen, and we could trade our going-home-on-leave money for bus and ski passes.

All this in between seeing Helena, of course. It had been quite difficult to see her as much as I had wanted. I remember we wrote lots of letters – love letters, I suppose you would call them. I loved writing them as much as getting them. But it was hard to actually talk very often.

'Only one phone line, and it's always engaged,' she'd say despairingly. And it was true. It's hard to imagine in these days of being in touch all the time, when everybody has mobile phones, but back in the day you had to queue to make a call – we had to fight for phone time. No wonder some young relationships fell by the wayside.

Not ours, though. However many things were taking up our time – and Helena, still at school, had plenty of studying to do in between her riding and soccer and all her other sports – we still made time to be together. It was serious between us, and we knew it.

Meanwhile, I went to ski instructor school in Jarpen, not far from Åre, the biggest ski resort in Sweden. The plan was for Helena to come and join me as soon as she had finished her studies, and together we'd do sport and think about the future.

As part of my new grown-upness, I also started to do some further studies – the idea was to take those exams I hadn't quite managed to pass when I was at school. Helena would work with me and together we'd set ourselves up for earning money and generally being together in the outside world.

But perhaps my skiing was a bit like my hockey. Perhaps someone should have told me I wasn't in the top league. In that first year I did get a bit downhearted. In fact, what I didn't know then was that some of the guys I was skiing with would go on to be top-class internationally famous skiers. All I knew then was that they were better than me.

But I was lucky to be doing what I enjoyed so much, I did realise that. I was also coming to realise that I was never going to do what everyone else did. Even with some exams under my belt, I think I was always going to go out there and do what I wanted to do, not get 'a job', not do what others told me to do.

One day I'll have an answer to the question 'What are you going to do when you grow up?'

But there was a new snag, as is so often the way. While I really just wanted to ski all day – especially ski-mountaineering, where you climb uphill with 'skins' on your skis – the truth was that being a ski instructor meant you had to instruct. And sometimes the people you had to instruct were very young. In fact, they were children. I just didn't have the patience for it. I wanted to test myself with the best, and slowing down and explaining to beginners was nowhere near where I wanted to be.

All this seems another world away now; these days, with very small children of my own, I have discovered infinite patience. I will take them through anything and everything they want to do – if they do want to do sport, that is; of course, they don't *have* to do anything – and I will love doing it slowly and carefully. But back then I was young and competitive and only wanted to be the best and be with the best.

But I had also begun to discover the sport that was going to hook me in for life – adventure racing. As an adventure racer, you are doing things like running, cycling or kayaking, in teams, non-stop over a period of days. Which I reckon makes adventure racing the ultimate test of mind and body. The basic principles are relatively simple, but logistically complicated: your team, usually made up of three men and one woman, has to get from A to B (and B can be hundreds of kilometres from A) by bike, on foot, in kayaks, sometimes abseiling, sometimes rock climbing or swimming. The clock starts on day one, and doesn't stop until you either fall by the wayside or cross the finish line, sometimes over a week later. So time is of the essence – and sleeplessness becomes more and more of an issue.

Nowadays there are endurance races all over the world all year round as part of the Adventure Racing World Series, but the climax of the year is the World Championship in November. This is when the very best teams have to be at the absolute top of their game, for the race is held in some of the world's most unwelcoming terrains – from desert to snow – and is 600–800 kilometres long. This means that even those who achieve the fastest times will have raced for nearly 120 hours, or five days, on only a handful of hours' sleep.

A good adventure racer has a rare combination of skills. Apart from the obvious need to be pretty fit, the most important thing, in my view, is loyalty. The team of four has to be together throughout the race – physically within five metres of each other. So the team has to act as one, literally and metaphorically. They have to agree on crucial decisions, and support each other. And that support can mean anything and everything. If, for instance, one of the team is going slowly, perhaps because they are finding the altitude difficult, then other, stronger team members can help them by towing them on bikes, or while running. Or, if someone is really sick or injured, by carrying them if necessary. You share your food and your water, and you encourage and support each other if – or rather when – exhaustion sets in.

You can have no outside help other than essential medical care and supplies at the transition area/TA. The TA is where you change from one discipline to another – from, say, trekking to biking. So you have to make sure your bikes are boxed up and in good condition for that stage – it's your responsibility to ensure you've got all the right equipment ready to be transported to the TAs. You have to make sure your equipment is the right type and weight and quantity (whether it's the weight of the bike box, or the silver blankets, or the energy bars), so you need to be extremely organised and forward-thinking. All navigation has to be done by map, so at least one of you has to be a good navigator. (No surprise that I'm only second navigator in our team.)

And then you have to plan your tactics at every stage – especially the question of when you sleep. Or *if* you sleep – some teams will decide to stop for two hours' rest at a time, others will crack on through the dark. So you have to be a clever, flexible tactician. Sleeplessness not only slows you down, but it can also make you halluci-nate, so however anxious you are to get to the front of the race, you have to have *some* rest, and planning that is key.

Added to all this, of course, is the fact that the big races take place in a mixture of very uncomfortable parts of the world – mountains, ice, jungle, rapids, rocks – and sometimes surrounded not just by mud and rain and waterfalls but also venomous snakes and insects. It's also entirely likely that you will be at high altitude and the temperatures will range from freezing to a humid forty degrees.

And so, of course, you also have to be very fit. Not just sprint fit so you can run or bike fast when the going's easy, not just upper-body fit so you can drag yourself across ravines on ropes or paddle through rapids, but also mentally fit and strong to withstand the sleep deprivation and the hundred other pains and discomforts that go with doing adventure sports in gruelling environments for days on end.

It is not everybody's cup of tea.

In fact, I would say that normal people – and most people are normal people – cannot even understand what motivates us to put ourselves through such an extreme form of . . . well, normal people would say 'torture'.

But I love the sport for all these reasons: how it tests you, how it pits you against yourself as well as the other teams. For me, to win a championship would be worth untold gold. If someone offered me the choice of a bag of two-million dollar notes, or to stand on the World Championship podium, I would pick the podium any day.

I used to try to explain this to people, to explain how I think of myself – and everyone involved in the sport – as having a different kind of 'comfort bubble'. I would say that mine is much larger than most. That is to say, most of the time people know the limit of what they can do, and for many people that might be a marathon, but for us a marathon is just the first day of seven. Many people would regard a trip in a canoe as a bit of an adventure. They see dangers all around them. But because I know the limit of what I can do, I see danger as something much further out.

I've raced for four days in Costa Rica on one hour's sleep. I've raced for seven days with most of my right heel missing. I've raced for six days with toes black from frostbite (and won the race). I've hallucinated, and I've tasted the metallic taste in my mouth that's a sign of the body shutting down.

My 'comfort bubble' is enormous compared to pretty well anyone else's, because if it's not as bad as those things, then it's fine. And this is what normal people don't understand.

And actually, I understand that they don't understand.

In Åre Helena and I were living the dream outdoor sporting life – paying our way with me teaching skiing, Helena working for a sports equipment company, and both getting more and more involved in racing. In 1999 we got our first major sponsor for the team, Reebok. I think that was pretty much the moment I decided Yes, I can do this. I can get people to buy in to what we do.

It wasn't long after that that we found ourselves in Switzerland, staying with my parents who were working out there. As people who were starting to be part of the fabric of Swedish adventure racing, we went to help Team Silva, the national team, at the first Adventure Racing World Championship in 2001. I remember standing next to my friend, Jari Palonen, now a famous adventure racer, and saying, 'I will never stand on the sidelines of an adventure race again. Next time I will be on the start line.'

I think he looked at me a bit sceptically, but I meant it. And indeed from there on in, we made adventure racing our goal, and our job. We worked hard, we made ends meet and we loved what we did.

But working all day to pay for our racing, and then exhausting ourselves racing, started to take its toll, and we found ourselves getting very tired as well as broke. It had become very difficult to keep it all together. So that year, 2001, to have a break and save a bit of money, Helena and I moved back to Örnsköldsvik and went to live on her parents' farm.

Their farm was a beautiful place with a beef cattle herd, a couple of dairy cows and some pigs and arable land. There were two farmhouses, one belonging to her parents, the other to her uncle. So family gatherings were huge events, involving not just Helena and her brother and parents – at harvest time we were twenty round the table most of the time.

And it was a wonderful family to be with. I often think that Helena's childhood – growing up surrounded by animals as she was – was a great start in life. She had responsibility for milking the cows, and had lots of pets to look after. And if you're taught to look after animals, to respect them and work with them, then I think it makes you better at being with people.

My childhood hadn't been like that at all – we never had pets, we certainly never had a dog . . .

But while I appreciated how worthwhile and good it all was, I did actually find the unrelenting predictability of farming life a bit wearing. I helped with the harvest, of course I did, but there was something in me that often thought, I would hate to know that I'd be doing this, in just the same way at just the same time, next year, and the year after that and the year after that . . .

In just the same way, I know Helena's father didn't get what I was trying to do. I had a part-time job as a personal trainer at the Örnsköldsvik training centre, but the important thing for Helena and for me was our adventure racing. We had just taken on the task of organising the first High Coast race – a gruelling course covering nearly 400 kilometres, involving teams of four racing non-stop. It involved a lot of work, getting sponsors, setting up a new website and organising the logistics.

And all this labour-intensive work made it impossible in the end for us both to do two jobs at once. In 2004 I gave up work at the gym, and Helena and I concentrated full-time on racing – as 'Team Explore' when we were competing, and as 'Explore Sweden' when we were organising races. We had an office in town, and we moved back there to be closer to work. And we set about organising an airborne Adventure Racing World Series race that featured a Boeing 737 flying the racers between three different destinations.

It was sensational, and a great race. The only slight snag was that we lost rather a lot of money. But thank goodness for sympathetic bank managers. And because we had one of those, we got a loan, got rid of the office and learned a valuable lesson as we set about planning the next World Series adventure race.

If the 2004 race had been exciting, then our race for 2006 was even more so. We were determined to make our race the best – to make it fun, not just challenging; and we were also determined to show Sweden and Norway at their best. But first there was the small matter of getting married.

We were always going to get married, no question of that, but we wanted it to be special and at a time when we were a bit more settled in our lives. January 2006 was the moment, and the beautiful church next to my parents' house the place. My mother had always been very involved in the church, and I think there'd always been a kind of unspoken assumption that we'd get married in this spot.

It all went fantastically. Helena looked beautiful, we all said the right words at the right time, all the family and our friends were there, there was laughter and happiness in all the right places. And the sun shone. Which, ironically, was a shame because that meant there wasn't any snow for our specially commissioned ski sleigh to take us to the reception on the mountain. We had to make do with old-fashioned wheels to make the journey up the mountain.

But if that's all that goes wrong with your wedding, well, I guess you're very lucky.

There wasn't much time for a honeymoon, though, because we had to get straight on with planning our special race – it takes pretty much a year to get everything right for a major AR World Series race. Eventually we were ready. And as the day dawned, there was nothing more we could do but hope for lots of entrants and that everyone would enjoy it.

And enjoy it they did. We were so proud of this race. As the winner said: 'Often organisers try to make the race so tough and brutal, almost as if they want to frighten people away from adventure racing. But here, any one of the sections would have been great to do any day, any week. To put twenty different experiences like that in one package is pretty awesome. We saw the Northern Lights while we were paddling, we saw whales, we saw reindeer. It was very special.'

What was a bit less special is that some of the sponsors who were meant to support the event didn't materialise. And because the previous year's World Championships hadn't been a great success, we found ourselves with fewer entrants than normal. All in all it was another climb up the learning curve . . . we had to become more brutally realistic about how we paid for what is, after all, an expensive sport.

I determined to handle everything myself from then on, sponsors and all. And while I would call around getting sponsorship, Helena would do the same for the media, and do all the paperwork.

We were a team. In a good way, and in every possible sense.

Chapter 3

Getting Peak Performance Fit

'Sometimes I look in the mirror and I think: "Not good enough, not fit enough." And when I see that, I know I need to put more energy in, more fight, to suffer.'

Örnsköldsvik, 2015

'Crayfish, ice cream, cheese, bananas, lingonberries, cinnamon buns . . . what else?'

Helena is getting ready for another visit to the shops. Which, with five mouths to feed, seems to have to happen pretty well every day.

Only half concentrating on the question, I look out of the window of the sitting room and watch Arthur having a deep sniff of his favourite corner of the garden. I see his tail wagging with excitement. It's a big, powerful tail, and happily, these days, it does a great deal of wagging.

Idly I wonder what it is that has set it off quite so energetically. And then I get it. He's in the corner where we have our barbecues. Somewhere in that patch of grass, invisible to us mere humans, there must be a minute trace of chicken thighs. This has turned out to be Arthur's favourite food in the world, especially when grilled on a barbecue. Who would have thought that a dog born and brought up in the grimmest of circumstances in the middle of the Ecuadorian jungle could have a taste for food that wouldn't be out of place at an English dinner party?

'Chicken thighs!' I shout to Helena. 'We'll have a barbecue tonight, so we've got to have Arthur's favourite.'

We do spoil him, but I think he deserves it. Eventually we're ready. We just need to get Arthur into the back of the car. I go into the garden, put on his going-shopping lead and together we walk to the car.

'Right then, Arthur. Up you jump,' I say to him in my sternest voice. Because I've a pretty good idea of what's going to happen next.

Arthur looks up at me as if butter wouldn't melt. His big amber eyes look slightly puzzled in an oh-so-polite way. *What?* he seems to be saying. *Me? Jump into the car? Why would I do that when I've got you to lift me up into it?*

I stare back at him. This happens every time. Arthur is actually an incredibly athletic dog – he can jump up on to a table from a standing start, a bit like a Harrier Jump Jet. And if I'm not around, if it's just Helena who's taking him shopping, he is perfectly capable of jumping into the car.

I carry on staring at him. 'Go on,' I say. 'Up you get.'

Arthur carries on staring back at me. He looks so beautiful and trustworthy. But I KNOW he's manipulating me!

I do know that. But hey, the next thing I know is that I am bending down, putting my arms round him and lifting him up. His head turns towards me, and I feel a little lick on my face as I put him gently into the back of the car.

He's done it again.

Örnsköldsvik, October 2014

Since there's nothing normal about adventure racing, it is not surprising that the team's shopping list for an Adventure Racing World Championship couldn't be further away from a normal shopping list. It's not only full of obvious things like gloves, helmets, energy bars and socks; it also has more unusual stuff like the silver blankets you cover yourself with if you're freezing cold or in deep shock, duct tape, waterproof matches and mosquito nets. Anything can happen on an adventure race, and you have to have the kit to be prepared for it. Over the years, I have learned that it can save precious seconds, as well as sore bums or feet, if you have exactly the right equipment in the right place.

But that October, our Ecuador Championship shopping list was more complicated than ever. We knew we were going to be in every variation of climate, and from what we could guess from the race information we were told before the start (the actual course is a secret until you get there), every variation of terrain.

And this race was extra hard because we were only allowed two boxes each, including the bike boxes, and their weight restrictions were unusually strict. We couldn't go over twenty kilograms on our gear, or twenty-five kilograms on our bike boxes. That's not a lot, when you have to account for race shirts, helmets, socks (it's important to have several pairs of socks; foot rot is a real problem after a few days on the run and in the wet), gloves, bandages, different sorts of shoes, bike pumps, towing lines, shorts, seat pads, mosquito nets, climbing harness . . . I could go on. But it's so knife-edge that you have to weigh everything, down to the spare batteries for your helmet lights. The rules are not designed just to make our lives difficult; they're also designed so that the boxes are light for the volunteers to carry from TA to TA. Still, it means huge added pressure on us to get things right – which is why the teams have two days just to pack after they arrive and before the race starts. They have to make sure each box for each TA has got exactly the right things in it, so the logistics can be hugely complicated.

And this is all before you begin to think about food supplies. All of which have to be planned according to the stage of the race. So you can eat 'normal' food if you're cycling in reasonable conditions, or you can maybe eat twenty-four-hour energy meals (which can be warmed up by a special thermal sleeve) in the kayak stretches, but only energy bars if you're running. I've been planning races for so many years now that I know how to do these lists with my eyes shut. But there was once a time when, in the middle of a twelve-hour trek, we arrived at a small village exhausted and found we had no food at all. There was just one rubbish bin by the side of the road. We scrabbled frantically inside it, and were rewarded with some sodden energy bars a previous team had thrown away. They were the most delicious energy bars we had ever eaten. But I swore to myself that I must never let that happen again.

Plus there was another consideration: we were going to go from zero to thirty degrees in the course of the race, so that aspect would be like the challenge of packing for a skiing holiday and a beach holiday all in one go. For us it meant fleeces and tights (yes, for the boys too – you need to protect your legs) as well as T-shirts and sunscreen.

We were going to be racing for 700 kilometres, or 435 miles. Made up of 158 kilometres of trekking /climbing / abseiling, 412 kilometres of biking and 128 kilometres of kayaking. Estimates were that the winners would take about 110 hours, and the maximum qualifying finishers would take up to 190 hours. Or eight days and nights of racing.

We would start the race at over 4,000 metres altitude, twice going down to around 2,000 metres and twice back up to 4,000 before ending at a place called Mompiche at sea level.

Even if you didn't count the additional hazards of venomous spiders and snakes, monsoons, ice, jungle and white water, it was going to be a challenging race, and we were going to have to train for it harder than ever before.

Örnsköldsvik, 28 October 2014, D-Day Minus 3

Faster! Higher! Colder!

It was now well into autumn in Örnsköldsvik. The bright sun on the lake looked beautiful and like the best sort of advertisement for the High Coast. No leaves on some of the trees, but the firs and spruces made up for that, and everything looked crystal-clear in the cold light of day.

My good friend and training partner Robert and I were halfway through our bike run to the top of the hill in Skagsudde. Robert was going fast, just ahead of me. He's a very good athlete, whose speciality is cross-country skiing, and when I'm level with him, or better than him, on these training sessions I know I'm in good shape.

The secret of these lung-busting, leg-crunching climbs is determination. Sheer grit. As it was all about being in peak condition in just two weeks' time, I needed a work-out not just for the legs, but also for the mind.

I looked down at my new state-of-the-art watch. To the untrained eye, it looked just like a blue diving watch, but actually it measured every breath and beat and kilo-metre. 158 beats, 28 km/h. Not bad. Could do better.

I pushed harder. The hill was steep, but the road was smooth, so there was no excuse for not hitting 30 km/h. One extra push and I got there. Edging past Robert on the corner I felt a rush of satisfaction. It wasn't actually a race, but it felt very like one.

Stopping at the top, lungs grabbing every available bit of oxygen – maximum heartbeat, maximum oxygen – I felt pretty great about this tough training for the legs.

'Good enough?' said Robert as he came to a stop. He's lean as a whippet, and it amused me how the super-slim-line Peak Performance shirt I'd given him seemed to have room to spare on him.

'Never good enough,' I answered. 'Let's hit the gym.'

We had a date to watch the hockey at the sports stadium where I used to work. It had a small but very effective gym club at the top of it, with a glass wall where you could watch the game as you burned your lungs out on the bikes and weight-lifting machines. Watching real people tear around the arena, with real people cheering them on, was better than any television, I reckoned.

Moments later we were there and getting out of the outdoor kit and into our indoor shorts and training tops. The gym manager came by as I finished putting on my shorts.

'Nice legs, Mikael,' he said.

I told him in a friendly fashion where to put himself. In fact, it's very practical to shave your legs – it means cleaning up wounds and scratches is easier and safer. I don't think you're a proper biker if you don't shave your legs. I took off my outdoor biking socks to get ready for indoor work. As I took my left sock off I saw what my beloved daughter had done the previous day. In love with a small pot of pink nail varnish, she had insisted on painting all our toenails bright pink.

Looking down at my feet I did wonder how many other adventure racers were quite so well-manicured on their training sessions.

Örnsköldsvik Airport, 31 October 2014

Örnsköldsvik Airport is not much more than a tower and an area of concrete that interrupts the forests. The luggage comes in on one belt through a hole in the wall, and goes out on another belt that passengers have to load up with their luggage themselves. The passport check is one person, or occasionally two for a busy flight. It's a long way, in every sense, from the busy hub that is Stockholm or Heathrow.

We arrived there that cold October evening a bit tense with everything that we still had to do, but excited that at last we were setting out on our Ecuador challenge, and that soon we'd be on the other side of the world ready for one of the most important races in all our careers.

The first thing that lay ahead of us was six days of getting used to the high altitude. We would be trekking and climbing in the mountains near Quito – and hoping that none of us were going to get too exhausted by the thin air. High altitude is tough on adventure racers, especially those of us who live at sea level and are not used to it. When your body is already stretched to breaking point, having limited oxygen can make the difference between life and – if not exactly death, then at least a near-death experience. So it helps to have time to get the body used to the idea.

For the first four days after arriving in Ecuador, we were going to be the Three Musketeers – our teammate Karen was only joining us for the last day as she was already used to high altitude at her home in Lake Tahoe.

As we milled around the small airport entrance, I looked at my teammates. First there was Staffan, looking like the stereotypical fit Swedishman. Tall and blond and, they say – I wouldn't know – handsome. He was larking about with the girl on the passport desk. We had so much enormous luggage, so many boxes that even if we weren't being noisy it would have been impossible not to notice us.

Then over in the other corner, checking and rechecking his bike boxes, there was Simon. Tall, dark and lean, he's a great athlete. Very fast, very keen to get there first. At twenty-five, he's the baby among us, but he's already going places. Fast.

Together with Karen, one of the world's toughest and most experienced adventure racers, we made up a good mix of skills. Plus we knew each other very well, and we knew how to support each other. As Simon says, 'It's really important to be good friends – we have a good time training, and we have a good time after training.'

Last on the plane was Krister Göransson, our photographer. Krister comes from the same town as me and has been a friend for over fifteen years. He's been taking photographs ever since he was six years old; it's the one constant in his working life. He's a fantastic photographer – and friend – and he's particularly brilliant not just at the scenic shots but also the action shots in adventure racing. Over the years he's had to get into some pretty uncomfortable positions to get the best pictures, but that's what he's good at.

As he chatted to the airport security staff, I could see that his cameras were going to take up almost as much room as our stuff. They were using up all our emergency allowance.

I walked over to him. 'I really hope,' I said, 'that you're going to take some bloody brilliant pictures with all this gear and extra cameras.'

He gave me a friendly V-sign.

Eventually it was time to give Helena and little Philippa a farewell hug. Helena would be following our progress every step of the way. Once the race started we would take the form of a small blob on her computer screen as our trackers sent signals back to the organisers.

Together with our friends Mia and Malin, Helena would be in charge of all the updates on Facebook and our websites, as well as all the paperwork that went with getting us all safely out to the other side of the world.

'Have a good trip,' she said. 'Ring me when you get there.' I always did ring her, as soon as I could once I'd arrived anywhere, or as soon as I finished a race. But I think she always feels she has to give me my instructions just in case I forget.

Eventually we were in the jet and heading to Stockholm for the connection to Amsterdam and from there to Quito, Ecuador. It was a pretty basic plane, with propeller engines. Noisy and rather windy. I idly wondered how I'd be feeling on the return trip in three weeks' time – would we be celebrating a victory? Or feeling sorry for ourselves for not being in the top ten? Or, worse still, not finishing? The familiar knot of tension that I always feel on the way to a big race got a little bit tighter.

The short flight to Stockholm was just the beginning of what was to be a big, long flight. When we arrived at Stockholm that evening we only had a few hours till our next flight to Amsterdam, so we checked into an airport hotel that was pretty much just a bunk bed and a door. Most people would think it too basic, but for us we knew it was the lap of luxury compared to what was coming soon. We made a point of going straight to sleep; we needed all the sleep we could get.

The following morning we hit the decks at dawn for the two-hour flight to Amsterdam. The next leg to Quito was thirteen hours, and once we were on the plane I reckoned we should use some of that time to talk strategy for the race. I knew we'd do this again when we caught up with Karen, but I wanted to get our tactics straight in my head.

'OK guys,' I said when we were settled in our seats at Amsterdam, next stop Quito. 'Let's get this straight. It's a tough start. First four stages have three climbs of two or three thousand metres with two drops of fifteen hundred and 4,000 metres. Two treks, two bikes. If we're lucky we can make it in thirty-six hours. Daylight is 5.30 a.m. to 6.30 p.m. so it should be simple to work out the dark zones, and get to TA4 without a break.' (The Transition Areas are key points in the race when you change from one discipline to another.) 'If we don't make any navigation mistakes.' I looked at Staffan.

He was pretending to concentrate on his peanuts, so I decided not to do any Getting Lost teasing.

'It depends on where we are in the daylight,' I went on. 'But if we get it right we could arrive at TA4, have a couple of hours' sleep and move on to the trek from there. But that leg is after 144k of biking so we would have to do that super-fast.'

I looked again at the others. Simon was looking at the altitude chart with a slightly concerned frown. There's no rhyme or reason why some people are affected by altitude and some aren't, but perhaps he was worried that he might be one of those who found high altitude difficult.

'But the main thing is,' I said a little bit more loudly because this was important, 'that we push on after Stage Six. That's 160k of biking, no more high altitude and that's where we can come out on top. This is about bike skills. It's our stage.'

They were looking at me properly now.

'It's very, very important where we are at Stage 7,' I went on. 'We go super-fast into the boats – doesn't matter if we're tired because we'll be downstream at that point.'

I'd been studying the tide charts, and if we got to the river by when I thought we could then we'd have a great advantage. 'What do you think about having just a ten-minute TA here? We arrive, just put our bikes in the box, continue in bike clothes – just keep everything on – grab food and lifejackets and go. Then we take twenty-four-hour meals in the boats and take a sleep at TA8, the bike stage, or 9, the trek stage, if we dare. We can do power naps.'

I had their attention now. I could see they understood that this last part of the race was absolutely make-or-break for us.

'Then we have a super-fast TA at TA9. Just keep all our running clothes on. Run to the boats with paddles, no loose items, maybe just keep backpacks on throughout these stages. So we transition in just five minutes!'

'OK,' said Staffan. His peanuts were finished so he had no excuse not to be concentrating. 'I can go with that. Sleepless high altitude for the first half. All-out race at the end.'

'And we mustn't worry about altitude,' I said, even though I was worried about altitude. 'We've got six days at high altitude before the race starts. We'll have climbed three mountains at over 4,000 metres. We'll be OK.'

Because that's what you have to do as captain. You have to say it'll be OK, and then somehow you just have to make it OK.

Day three of acclimatising in Ecuador and I was right. It gave me no satisfaction to know that, but still, I was right. We were not great at altitude.

We were three of the toughest guys you could wish to meet on a mountain, but the last two days, climbing Ruminahui and Illinizas, both over 4,000 metres above sea level, we had all suffered. We were climbing higher and higher as fast as we could and still getting deeply breathless. It's a strange sensation, using up huge amounts of energy and not getting very far. You can't really overcome it by willpower either.

We were being led by a charming Ecuadorian guide, who assured us today's climb would be easy. So Krister was going to come with us, take some shots of the sensational Ecuadorian mountains, and maybe make a video for the sponsors back home.

The first part went smoothly enough. We were in our arctic kit – boots, poles, the lot – and were halfway up the mountain when Krister said, 'Stop, this is the place.' We were going to make a movie. All very well, I thought, but we are all so breathless none of us can actually speak properly. The combination of racing uphill and the high altitude – we were nearly at 4,000 metres at this point, quite a lot higher than Quito – had pretty much deprived us of the power of speech.

Still, Staffan, as the most robust in the thin air, gave a pretty good impression of someone who could talk. And after he'd done his piece to camera we moved on, determined to make it to the summit and crack the 4,000-metre mark.

At that moment I heard a distant shout. 'Mikael! Hey there, Mikael!' At first I couldn't see where the shouting was coming from, and then I spotted four figures coming towards us.

It was Nathan Fa'avae's wife (Fa'avae is captain of the New Zealand Seagate team) and their three small children. They were kitted out like they were on a beach holiday. And they were bouncing around as if they *were* on a beach.

We waved hello and watched them run on down the mountain in their beachwear. They must have come down from well over 4,000 metres. I swore inwardly. They looked superhuman, and there we were, in full arctic rig, really suffering. Seagate were the favourites to win the race, and they sure looked like they had a head start with acclimatising to the altitude.

'OK,' shouted our guide half an hour later. He was ahead of us, and had none of the problems breathing that we had. 'That was it, turn round now.'

We were puzzled. Surely we should get to the top first? Surely that was the point?

'Big storm coming,' our guide said by way of explanation. 'Turn round now.' He sounded pretty sure. We all looked around and saw nothing out of the usual, no sign of even a dark cloud.

Then suddenly: 'There it is!' shouted Simon. 'He's right. God, look at that.'

We all turned round, and there in the distance we could see that the sky had turned completely black and seemed to be heading our way.

The guide led us down towards a ridge. He was – rather unnervingly – running. 'Hurry, hurry,' he shouted at us. And we could see that he was starting to follow a path that was marked with flags he must have planted on the way up, knowing we might be heading for a storm.

'Come on,' he said to us all. 'We need to run.'

Krister, holding his cameras close to him protectively, said to him, 'No. I don't do running.'

The lightning was getting more frequent now, and it was starting to hail. By this time the lightning seemed to be getting closer and closer, and we were getting even more breathless from the thin, electric atmosphere. We put our helmets on to protect us from the huge hailstones, which by now were as big as grapes. And then we saw lightning strike right in the middle of the trail we had nearly gone down a moment ago.

It was just the spur our photographer needed, and

together we ran as fast as we could down to the bottom and the safety of the hut. As we started to get out of our soaking kit, I saw that the electricity had completely destroyed my phone.

I sure hoped all this training would prove worthwhile when it came to the race.

Chapter 4

They're Off!

'We're all in this together'

Höga Kusten, July 2015

Staffan and I are in a hurry. The High Coast Swim/Run that we're scoping out and organising is only days away, and we still need to work out the route of the second half. It's just as gruelling planning a race as it is competing in it. In fact, a bit more so, because it's easy to make mistakes and follow a route that proves too dangerous and difficult for the official race.

It's well into the afternoon and we're on our seventh climb. I look up at the rocks ahead of me to check on the progress of our chief scout. Looking rather fetching in his life jacket, Arthur is padding confidently across the top of the trail.

So far today he's been taking the lead. He always seems to be able to tell which direction we are heading in, and he goes in front in that way that he has when he wants to know what's round the corner. But all the time, he's one of us; even in the difficult bits, his attitude is one of 'We're all in this together.'

This bit of mountain is extra rocky and super-steep. As I look up at him, I can see what Arthur can't. The trail leads to a sheer face of rock and comes to a dead end.

All day, Arthur's been right there with us, doing everything we do, whether it's in the water or on the rocks. But as he comes round the corner and sees the rock face he comes to a stop. From below, I can see him sniffing the edges and the slope of the rock. He can't go forward and he can't go back.

He's in a pickle. But he doesn't seem to be worried. He just stands still, and then a moment later he looks down. He's looking at me as I climb towards him as if to say, *Take your time, I've got all day.*

I can hear Staffan climbing behind me. As we get nearer to Arthur I can see that we're both going to have to carry him up over the sheer bit of rock. Staffan can see what I'm seeing, and has come to the same conclusion – much as he would in a race; it's why we work so well together. Arthur doesn't take his eyes off me, and as I get close, he looks down at me with his usual trusting expression. He looks at Staffan in the same way as Staffan joins us on the ledge.

Staffan climbs past us both and scrambles to the top of the trail. I start to pick up Arthur to pass him up to Staffan. As I lean over and take hold of thirty kilos of golden dog, I can feel that Arthur is totally relaxed. He's looking around him as if to say, *This is interesting.*

And then, when I put him down, he carries on trotting up the mountain as if nothing had happened. It's as if he knows he's part of the team. He'll play his part. We play ours.

As he disappears over the top, I know he knows I won't be far behind. He thinks I will always be there to look out for him.

And so I will.

Quito, November 2014

They told us Ecuador has the most amazing biodiversity in the world, with more species of birds, mammals and reptiles than more or less any other country; that there are rare spectacled bears, monkeys, pumas, wolves and condors.

In the huge ecological reserves and jungles, they said, there are some of the highest volcanoes in the world, where you can admire the evidence of lava flows around some of the biggest lakes, which are famous for giant trout and electric eels.

They told us that the waterfalls and mysterious caves were infinitely picturesque, and that the wetlands were a paradise for orchids and vines. And they told us that you could find hummingbirds, otters and monkey frogs in the rivers, and biting ants, vampire bats and poison-dart frogs in the swamps.

But just two days before the start of the race, we had other things on our minds than flora and fauna. We came down from the mountains to meet Karen for one last climb before packing for the race. Racu Pinchincha was 4,700 metres, so that was good practice for us all. And then, after that, there was no more time for practice or looking out for rare plants and animals; it was the real thing in just two days' time, and we needed to head for the hangars and start a day of packing.

It was a weird sight: the old Quito Airport, a vast abandoned hangar, now alive again. But this time, instead of baggage belts and tired passengers, now it was humming with the chatter of athletes, surrounded by plastic bike boxes and racing gear.

All around I could hear muttering in unintelligible languages, and occasionally the 'hi hi' of a friendly greeting. Adventure racing is a small world, and of the 200-odd athletes gathered there on that Friday morning, I could probably say 'hi' to most of them.

But this wasn't the time for social chit-chat. Everyone was utterly focused on the piles of plastic boxes in front of them – in between them were bike wheels, packs, food and all the endless essential kit we knew would be make-or-break at some point over the next eight days. No wonder they gave us two days for the process.

Eventually, when everything was packed and the boxes loaded up and wending their way to the transition areas, we set off for Quito's central square and the opening ceremony.

This bit of the old town, dating from the Spanish colonial era, is a UNESCO cultural heritage site. The picturesque cobbled square seemed a bit at odds with its brutal history; in the sixteenth century it was a battleground between the Spanish and the Inca warriors. The Incas in Quito had apparently held out against the Spanish for longer than anywhere else in the country, and had razed it to the ground rather than see it fall to the Spaniards. As someone once said, perhaps it's not surprising that some of the world's most beautiful countries have a troubled history – people fight over nice things.

But the only combat for now was between fifty-three lots of four athletes, all of us quiet and peaceful for the moment as we watched the opening ceremony – flags and music and dance – which was quite a spectacle on that cobbled square. Or it was until it was cut short by the heavens opening, the sudden downpour making us rush to the shelter of some nearby colonnades. It must have looked a rather bizarre sight – 200-odd endurance athletes rushing to escape a rain shower, like shoppers on Oxford Street who have forgotten their umbrellas. But once you're in a race, your immune system drops far below normal, so you can very easily get sick from getting wet and cold, and getting sick is a racer's worst nightmare.

But there was no escaping the rain, and we were all pretty damp as we sat in the Quito theatre afterwards waiting for the technical briefing. I suppose for normal people this would be another surreal sight. Endurance athletes seated in serried ranks in an old-style opera theatre, for all the world as if they were waiting for the overture to finish and Verdi's *La Traviata* to strike up.

In fact, we were all tense with apprehension, not just because our squelching dampness made us all worried that we'd get ill before we even started, but also because the announcement of the course couldn't happen too soon for us. We knew we would be crossing coastal, mountainous, Amazonian jungle terrain, and the equator. We knew the general directions, but until we had the course maps we couldn't really start planning. And with a 5 a.m. start the following day, the sooner we started analysing the maps and comparing them with tactics, the better. So just as soon as the organisers, Huairasinchi (which means 'the strength of the wind' in the native Kichwa language), issued the course maps, we rushed back to the hotel for a sleepless night of map-gazing, using different colours of highlighter pens to work out various possible routes. With such an early start we weren't going to get much sleep anyway so, like most of the teams, we used the time to plot and plan.

Day one of the race was shaping up to be a beautiful one. The buses that took us through the beautiful Antisana reserve drove slowly up the steep, winding roads. Which gave us plenty of time to admire this eastern part of the Andes highlands, with the snow-capped Antisana volcano and the even higher volcano, the famous Cotopaxi.

The four of us were sitting at the front of the bus; we had a perfect view.

'Isn't that so great?' said Karen, looking around at the spectacular views. Years of living in the States had given her a bit of an American accent. 'Great day. But I think we're going to get some crazy weather, don't you? Going to be a huge factor in the race.'

I looked at my teammate as she peered eagerly out of the window. She looked fitter and tougher than ever. She was a great person to have on your side.

Karen and I were sitting in front of Staffan and Simon, close enough to chat, but no one was saying anything much. This part of the race, the calm before the storm of the starting gun, was when we were all at our most tense. In fact, you could feel the tension emanating from everyone on the bus – although hardly anyone ever shows it, nerves can play a huge part for some racers at the beginning of a race. Sometimes people are so nervous they throw up.

When we arrived at the start line, we discovered an Ecuadorian brass band had got there first. As we were organising our maps and kit for the beginning of the race it was rather odd to have loud oom-pah drums and trumpets in the background. Looking around at the huge mountainous scenery, everyone agreed, though, that Ecuador had provided one of the most breathtaking settings for the first stage of a race.

Sometimes the start of a race can be a bit show-offy. Even though we had some 700 kilometres to race, you sometimes get competitors setting off as if they were running a 200-metre sprint. But this time I think the enormity of what was in store – and the high altitude – calmed everyone down. And the four of us jogged away from Laguna la Mica in good spirits and at a good speed.

This first trekking stage was only twenty-nine kilometres, but we were at high altitude, well over 4,000 metres, and the going got incredibly muddy. To start with the sun shone and the tracks through the forests were easy, but it wasn't long before we started to slow down. Rather disconcertingly, we saw other teams going in different directions, and as we tried to find the first checkpoint we were a bit lost and a bit more tired than we should have been.

It had been a beautiful start to the race – with massive views across the plain and the spectacular Antisana volcano in the distance – but by the time we'd found that first checkpoint we weren't in great shape. Not a good start, I thought, but didn't say out loud to the others. Bad route choices; we knew we weren't in the top ten, and were all a bit dispirited as we got to TA1 to change to the bike section.

For everyone else, though, there seemed to be a bit of a party atmosphere at the first transition area, with plenty of smiling Ecuadorian locals clapping us on as we came and went. It was still so early in the race, and everyone seemed to be enjoying the scenery.

Everyone else being cheerful didn't exactly help my mood; we now knew that our bad decisions meant we were over an hour behind the leaders. Definitely *not* a good start. But I knew this next stage involved bikes and a big descent, which I reckoned would go a long way towards making us feel better. Cycling downhill into thicker, warmer air was a pretty good thought.

We quickly got the bits of bike out of their boxes, put them together and without changing our clothes headed off down the track as quickly as we could. It was a bright, still day and the next leg was good going. The roads by the side of some of Ecuador's famous volcanic lakes were smooth enough for us to be able to admire the view as we cycled.

Within minutes we were feeling much better. The downhill, the biking, the thicker air were working their magic.

'We've got a treat coming up,' I shouted back to the others. Ahead of us was an actual road, Simón Bolívar Road, named after the Venezuelan revolutionary and South American hero of the nineteenth century. But this wasn't what I was excited about; it was the road itself. It was a smooth, properly tarmacked road that went on for thirty kilometres – and went down for 1,800 metres. We made the most of it, and chatted among ourselves as we pedalled more and more cheerfully.

Just as well we made the most of it, because only too soon we were knee deep in muddy, swampy trails that were hard to find and almost impossible to cycle on. It was just as well that all four of us were feeling better for losing so much altitude.

We leaned over the handlebars, gritted our teeth and just got on with it. Sixty-odd kilometres later and we were nearly at El Chacho and TA2, back on dirt track roads and going through some smatterings of the small concrete houses that made up the typical Ecuadorian villages.

As we came down a hill into a village called Jardín Gabriela Mistral we saw a guy on the side of the road who was scrubbing away at a couple of old cars. I guessed he was the nearest thing to a garage for miles around. I didn't spend long thinking about him because I was busy doing some maths in my head. I reckoned we'd made up good time on this leg, and might be only an hour behind the leaders.

Then Simon gave a shout. 'Hey, Karen!' he said. 'What's Spanish for can we borrow your hose?'

Karen knew a little Portuguese, and while that sometimes helped her to understand Spanish, I wasn't surprised to see her shake her head. But by this time Simon was off his bike and approaching the guy. He'd spotted what we hadn't – that Mr Garage had a spray hose.

'Cuánto?' I heard Simon say to him in his best cod Spanish. And he reached into his cycle shorts where he kept the Team Peak Performance emergency cash. He must have handed over quite a lot because it made Mr Garage smile broadly and nod.

Simon picked up the hose and directed a powerful blast at his mud-spattered bike. Brilliant. The mud shot off into the air, and his bike was now pretty much ready to pack up for the next leg. We all did the same thing, and soon our bikes were looking pristine.

'That's perfect, Simon,' I said. 'That'll save us a good fifteen minutes queuing at the TA.' If you pack up dirty bikes, sealing up the mud on the wheels and chains, there's a pretty good chance they'll be unusable when you next get them out.

I allowed myself the treat of fresh socks and a covering of Sportslick protection at this stop – rotting feet are a constant threat. And it's no joke to walk for days with the skin hanging off your heel. A grim image, but the reality was even worse . . .

There was lots of refuelling at this stage. The next trekking leg was going to be a bit tough – and back up to a high altitude – so we ate as many carbohydrates as we could: cake, pasta and noodles. And we made sure we had some of our special vacuum packed meatballs, the kind you can heat up with a cotton thermal sleeve.

It was good to be in tropical conditions after the grassy highlands of the beginning of the race. Plus I was feeling good as we marched off at a fast pace. This section started out on the famous El Chaco–Oyacachi trail, one of only three natural trails that link the western and eastern Andes. It started off on a dirt road within sight of the river, and as we overtook a number of other teams we started to feel even better.

It wasn't long before we came to the first man-made obstacle in among the natural ones. It took the form of a rotten bridge lying across the roaring rapids of the river. It looked dangerous – like 'falling through the rotten wood into the river below' dangerous. So the race organisers had installed a *via ferrata* – an iron wire that we were meant to attach to our harnesses – to make the crossing safe. There were no officials about, so Karen and Staffan decided to save time by not bothering to attach their harnesses. 'We can do it,' they said. 'Not a problem.'

They set off across the river – in the pouring rain, in the semi-darkness. Just as they had nearly finished crossing, the officials turned up. 'What the hell do you think you're doing?' they shouted.

'Hey,' shouted Staffan back. 'How were we to know? Where were you to tell us?'

I had watched, tensely, as they had edged across the roaring river. Sure, they were fine, but when it came to Simon's and my turn we put on our harnesses. The last thing we wanted was some sort of time penalty for bad behaviour.

From there on the going was tough and getting tougher. We were climbing again – the next TA was back up at over 3,000 metres – but this time in the mud and the rain and constantly climbing over roots and rocks and vicious vegetation and steep gullies. The pouring Amazonian rain started to feel cold as well as uncomfortable.

Finding the right path was a constant challenge; nothing in that sticky bit of jungle bore the slightest resemblance to anything you might call a path. We headed down towards the river, reckoning it couldn't be actually wrong to follow it. Climbing the paths alongside it, across fallen trees and abandoned barbed wire, made for very slow going. And it didn't help that we had a major climb until we got back to a dirt road. Tired as we were by this stage, we still managed to give a friendly wave to a cheery Ecuadorian woman who was herding her two cows ahead of her on the track.

We knew we were getting near the village when we saw another cheery Ecuadorian standing behind a stall. As we got nearer, we could see that she had rows of dark yellow bottles in front of her.

Another team was just heading off, clutching one of the bottles. Karen slowed down and said something to the woman behind the table.

'It's pure aloe vera juice,' she said, turning to the rest of us. 'This can only be a good thing. Come on, let's do it.'

Simon dug out his wallet again. Who knew it was going to have such a busy time in the middle of the jungle? And within moments we all had a glass of yellow liquid and the cheery Ecuadorian woman looked even cheerier.

The others took tentative sips and, with various expressions of disgust, put their glasses down. But I thought if a little is good for you, then a whole glass must be even better. Taking a deep breath, I put my lips to the glass and somehow got the whole lot down me. It tasted absolutely disgusting. Like glue.

We got back on our bikes and headed on to the transition area just as the dawn was breaking. I think it was probably a spectacular view, but I didn't really notice because at that point I suddenly needed to bend double in the middle of the road and painfully regurgitate a lot of bright yellow aloe vera juice. You can, apparently, have too much of a good thing.

As we fell into the transition area, I checked our time yet again. They reckoned this section should take between ten and twenty hours. We'd taken just over thirteen. Despite being at a low ebb and pretty exhausted, we were making good time. Mixed news for Sweden at that stage, though, as we heard that one of our great rivals, the Haglöfs Silva team, had had to pull out. The woman in the team, Josefina, had had a bad fall off her bike and broken her hand. It is impossible to continue in a race like this if you can't bike or paddle properly. Despite the careful control of the races, accidents absolutely will happen, but you never think it's going to happen to you.

The transition area was a large concrete platform, surrounded by tents and the odd hut. The TA was noisy, the blue pallet beds we had to lie on were rock hard, and there wasn't much room to lie out flat in between the bike boxes and equipment strewn all over the concrete ground. I was sore, tired and not feeling great in the higher, thinner air. But this was our first sleep in nearly twenty-four hours, and it was amazingly easy to lose consciousness.

Moments later, it felt like, we were up and getting set on our bikes. It was pouring with rain, a real tropical monsoon as we set off in the dawn. I began to sweat like a pig as we started the bike ride up the mountains – the feeling of being freezing cold only a few hours before seemed to belong to another world.

It felt good to start with, and I even spent a little time admiring the view again – this leg was 144 kilometres, most of it through the Sierra Highlands.

And, boy, were they highlands. As we biked up and up on the mountain track, I began to feel more and more rubbish. I was well behind the others – Staffan out front seemed to be entirely unaffected by the altitude and was biking strongly. Karen and Simon were doing OK, just behind him. But I was really starting to struggle. I looked at my odometer. It doesn't register any speed at all unless you are doing at least 3 km/h – which is pretty much a slow walk. And it wasn't registering any speed at all.

I shouted to the others, got off my bike and just lay by the side of the road panting. It felt like the veins in my head were bursting, and I couldn't do much more than lie there for a bit. We were now back up to nearly 4,000 metres, and I could feel every one of them.

'Hey,' said Staffan. 'No worries. I'll tow you.' And he attached his elastic bungee rope to my handlebars.

'Not sure this will work,' I said in between the panting. 'Let's try though.'

We set off again up the track, Staffan still moving strongly even though he was pulling an extra person and an extra bike. But I couldn't do it. Not even being pulled. We had to stop again and I took ten minutes sitting still by the side of the road.

'Not that much more,' said Staffan. 'Then it's downhill all the way.'

Drawing on all my reserves, I made it up to the highest point. But we were cold and soaking. There was now lightning and thunder to add to the rain, and as we began the descent it started raining even harder.

We stopped to consult the map. Whole chunks of it were almost solid brown with contour lines. When you think that one line equals forty metres we could see that we were in for some super-steep biking.

And then, somehow, we managed to get it wrong. After some hours we found ourselves on the wrong side of a thick bunch of contour lines. Anxious to avoid more uphill in our exhausted state than was absolutely necessary, we tried a route that looped round them. We ended up on precisely the opposite side of where we needed to be.

We found ourselves approaching a small village. Exhausted, cold and soaking wet, we saw there was a small school standing empty on the side of the road. As one, we dived inside and collapsed in a tired and depressed heap. We started to take some of our outer layers off in the hope that they would dry a bit. As I squeezed out a couple of pints of water from my jacket I reckoned we'd probably lost at least two hours on that last stretch.

But with no time to dwell on the thought of how many other teams had overtaken us – we were probably four hours behind the leaders by now – we got back on our bikes and headed on down what we thought was the right trail. After a big descent we approached what looked like an old railway track. As we got nearer, there was no doubt; we were back on the right route and it *was* a disused railway track. The clue being in the fact that the actual railway was still in place. Reassuring, but making for a bumpy ride.

All around us throughout this leg was an arid mountainous landscape, interspersed with the odd tall cactus. It seemed to be getting hotter and hotter, and then after yet another ascent we passed a brown sign welcoming us to the northern hemisphere. I guess if any of us had felt like it, we would have stopped and marked the occasion. It's not every day you cross the equator, after all. As it was, we just wanted to plough on and get on to the next stage. And given that it was now night-time there wasn't even the incentive of a view.

Getting to the next stage was easier said than done, as we realised that somehow we were missing Map 10, the crucial map to get us from the equator towards TA4. We knew we had to head north for about twenty kilometres, and that there were a number of forbidden roads on the way. Easy roads, which we were not allowed to use, were marked on the maps with red crosses. Accessing them would incur a penalty, which we could ill afford.

Suddenly Team Peak Performance became very sociable. We stood around by our bikes in the middle of a road leading out of the equator area. An American team hove into view. We said 'Hi' and 'How was the altitude for you?' They said hi back and asked if we'd lost our bearings. As they were a bit unsure of their route they got out their maps. Under the guise of helping them through their uncertainty, we all focused our minds and our headlamps on the map and managed to work out where we were. This lasted us for about another hour or two of biking, until we weren't sure of our bearings again. We had caught up with another team, and managed to do the same thing again. Who said adventure racing wasn't a sociable activity?

For much of the rest of this long and hard leg it was dark. It was a great relief to cycle into TA4, San José de Minas. The TA was humming with activity – and also with resentment. Plenty of the teams had made a mistake and, instead of keeping the river to their left as instructed, had crossed it too early. This was going to mean a four-hour penalty (where you have to take the penalty as compulsory rest) at the next transition area. And we had to pay that penalty even though I was convinced we hadn't made the mistake the others had.

I turned away from the arguing groups of racers and saw in the distance a rather great-looking church near the

TA, all lit up against the skyline. In another world I'd have taken time to admire the sight; but for now we had to get on with hosing down and oiling our bikes.

We knew we had some catching up to do; there was still everything to play for.

Chapter 5

Digging Deep in the Bucket of Pain

'I think suffering is a skill'

In the middle of the hum of activity, we decided to allow ourselves two hours of rest. Lying on the concrete floor, with people walking around inches from our heads, it was amazing that we managed to drift off. But nearly forty solid hours of extreme exercise can act more efficiently than any sleeping pill.

The next stage was a forty-five kilometre trek back up to three and a half thousand metres, so getting a bit of sleep under our belts seemed like a good idea. But we mistimed it, and I didn't come to until ten minutes into the third hour. The rules of sleep in adventure racing are that you have to sleep in one-hour stretches, so if you sleep even a few minutes over you can't get going until the next hour is up. So I decided we should continue sleeping for the next fifty minutes. Sleeping is a science in racing. In some races, there are so many rules to it (an obligatory eight hours throughout the race, a compulsory three hours here or there, penalties to be taken at specific TAs), that sometimes trying to work it all out is enough to keep you awake at night . . .

We set off from the TA at a sharp pace, almost running. The road was smooth and started off downhill; we were full of energy, and we were determined to move fast on this stage. With plenty of breath to spare, we started talking about our favourite breakfasts in the real world. Somehow talking about something that was nothing to do with the race was refreshing and relaxing.

The road started to climb, and then it totally disappeared, as roads had a way of doing in this country. There was nothing that looked anything like a path, so we plunged into the undergrowth, relying as ever on Staffan's map-reading. We climbed up and up, talk about breakfast having completely stopped by now, and found something that looked almost like a trail at the top of a ridge. It didn't feel right, but when we saw the checkpoint and knew we were on the right track, we had to hand it to Staffan – he was giving good guidance. But it was only the beginning of an even huger climb. There wasn't any thought of breakfast now. And not even a view to distract us; the low-lying clouds managed to hide whatever scenery there was.

Finally it was time to descend again. This time we knew we had to look for a real trail, the historic trail that the Inca warriors used to transport goods – the Cuchilla de los Olivos. We got a little way down the mountain before realising it was right in front of us. A path cut so deep into the mountainside that it looked like a First World War trench, with vegetation and mud growing high on either side. We set off down it, still in high spirits. Staffan was back on his breakfast jokes, and we were making fast progress.

The Ecuadorian team later told us that in the time of Prohibition, the trail was used by lowlanders to transport alcohol made from sugar cane – a drink called *canelazo* – up to the highland towns near Meridiano. There must have been a lot of trafficking – the trail was two or three metres deep in parts. At times the vegetation grew over the top of the trench, so it was like walking through a tunnel. A soft, shady tunnel, going downhill. We made the most of it.

A few hours later, and it was all a lot less comfortable. It was dark, it was raining, the mud was up to our knees and the trail had come to an end. Staffan's jokes had completely died out as he concentrated on navigating.

But the frequent pauses for him to focus his headlamp on our map paid off, and we got safely to the gravel track of the last stage. It was hot by now, brutally hot, so it was a relief to arrive at Meridiano, or TA5 as we knew it. Sixteen hours that section took. Not bad, but not good either.

As I looked around the transition area, I could imagine having a good hiking holiday in Meridiano, with or without a glass of *canelazo*. It was an almost Alpine-like village set on the side of a mountain, with a huge stone terrace where you could admire the view.

Beneath the terrace was a plain white stone church, which had been designated our transition area. The pews had been cleared away and stacked by the walls of the church. There were lots of locals around, and they didn't seem unduly perturbed by the sight of athletes sorting through their bike boxes under the altar. In fact, they probably welcomed us as a source of extra income – some of them were selling soup, rice and pork dishes at five dollars a pop. We succumbed, and Simon's TPP wallet came into its own again. The next leg was going to be one of the toughest, 160 kilometres of biking plus rope work over the water, and we reckoned we needed all the calories we could get. The time estimate for this stretch was somewhere between nineteen and thirty hours. That was a lot of hours in one go.

Full of pork, we settled down for our four-hour penalty sleep in a quiet corner under the Virgin Mary. Good food and the blessing of the Madonna might just give us a good start.

And for the first hour or two it looked like the pork and the Madonna were on our side. We were making smooth progress and the icing on the cake was our over-taking the Swedish Armed Forces team. Adventure racing is very competitive, but there's an extra edge when it comes to our compatriots. We gave them a friendly wave as we biked past them.

But things soon started to go downhill – metaphori-cally, but not at all literally. The going got steadily stickier and muddier. It was still dark and it was now raining, and it was a cold rain.

Usually at least one of us is up – physically and mentally – and can keep the rest of us going in the down times. But this time all of us were starting to struggle. Simon, always one to sprint at everything if he could, was quite subdued and going slowly. Staffan and Karen, both usually so strong, were obviously finding it tough too. Our route was going relentlessly up and down – no sooner had we painfully gained some altitude than we lost it again. And the ground was either thick vegetation and mud, or rocky mountain tracks.

Adding to the fun, my bike was starting to play up and started to be very reluctant to go into first gear, a pretty important gear when it comes to climbing steep moun-tain tracks. As I was struggling to make it work, having slowed almost to walking pace, I heard crunching noises behind me. Team Swedish Armed Forces. Absolutely powering up the hill and quickly overtaking us with a cheery wave.

We looked at each other grimly. Nothing needed to be said. And, at our lowest ebb, we carried on up the track. About an hour later, just as the sun was rising, cold and thoroughly exhausted, we got to a village. Not an Alpine-style village with a great view this time, but a poor Ecuadorian village with just a handful of dilapidated shacks with corrugated iron roofs. A mass of telegraph wires grew out of some of the walls, and piles of rubbish lay haphazardly over the ground. One of the buildings had tables outside it. An elderly guy and two women were hovering about in the background, and there were plates and mugs on the tables.

'OK,' I said. 'We need a break. We need food and a rest. We're not going to make it even to the rope stage if we go on like this.'

The abseiling and canyoneering wasn't due for another six or seven hours at least, but at this rate we wouldn't have the strength to cling on to the ropes. We had to take stock in every sense.

We got off our bikes and almost fell into four chairs at one side of the makeshift cafe. Karen's Portuguese some-how got through, and we were given a big pile of crack-ers, cheese and some rather mysteriously thick yoghurt. All of us set to as if we hadn't eaten in months. Which is exactly how it felt.

None of us said anything very much. I was feeling sore all over, and now had a new worry in the form of a sting-ing in my right eye. I could feel it was swelling up, and it was difficult to see out of the right-hand side of it. The shoulder I'd dislocated years ago was getting more and more painful, and my right knee – the one that had been badly sewn up in a tent in Finland during one race – was throbbing more than usual. There wasn't a muscle or a bone that hadn't had some twist or collision, and at times like this you could feel almost every one.

I looked at my teammates, my mates, my team, as they focused on their food. Shoulders rounded, silent, their cycling kit spattered with mud, gloves and packs lying discarded on the ground as if abandoned entirely in the moment of low despair. And I had a flashback to a morning years earlier and a coaching session with my floorball team. They were a bunch of eighteen-year-olds who I was meant to turn into a lean, mean fighting machine. But, like lots of eighteen-year-olds, they showed more enthusiasm for partying and girls than for scoring goals. After two successive defeats, I gave them the lecture of a lifetime, entirely inspired by Al Pacino in *Any Given Sunday*.

I told them we were 'in hell, and we could stay there or fight and climb our way out'. I told them that I couldn't do it for them, but that we'd heal as a team, or crumble as a team.

I gave it my all. It had the eighteen-year-olds jumping about the locker rooms with motivation; it was the beginning of a whole winning streak and a whole new seriousness. It was fantastically exciting to see them going from strength to strength.

I looked back at my teammates. No, I didn't think it would work now. This wasn't a time for cheerleading, just leading.

I got myself back into positive mode and stopped thinking about the injuries, my eye, the lost time, the broken gearbox – this was the moment to dig deep in the bucket of pain. I roused the team, and got us back on our feet and on our bikes. The next stage was going to be better.

We made it. Two hours later and we were at the waterfall. Somehow the sight of the rushing water and the ropes and zip wires energised us. After all the biking and trekking, this was a chance to play with some kit.

The Tyrolean traverse, or flying fox, or zip-wire . . . Whatever you called it, this was a dizzying, exciting flight across a canyon; you slid at huge speed down a wire, feeling as if you were heading to certain death, until the rope suddenly split into two directions, breaking your flight. We left our bikes at the roadside, since the rope section was by way of being a round trip, and they weren't going to come with us.

First we had to put on our harnesses, then jump in the river, just by the waterfall they called Salto del Tigre ('Jump of the Tiger'), then climb up to the zip-wire, fly down over the rapids, then up across slippery rocks and back up to a slack-line bridge that we had to cross holding on to an overhead wire. Just what we needed to wake us up, I said to the others.

And so it was – the exhilaration of feeling the air rush by as we jumped from high up on the rocks into the water, and then as we shot down the rope, made up for some of the hell of the last hundred kilometres. Not so much fun was walking on a slack line over the rapids – we could see each other's legs trembling with exhaustion as we concentrated on keeping a grip on the wire – but still, a welcome break. (Normal people would regard a welcome break as featuring a double bed and an en suite bathroom, I know.)

After our refreshing swim, the sun went down. So the last part of the leg was more hard work, on a bike, in the dark. And we made it especially hard work for ourselves when we got to a track that said 'Private'. Although it looked like the right route, we thought 'private' meant 'private' and doubled back, adding several kilometres to our route and lost another hour. To our annoyance, we discovered later that it had been the right route, and we racers had had the right to trespass.

The next stage was kayaking. We had three hours of dark zone to go before it would be light enough to get on the river, so we'd have an enforced sleep at the next TA – which would mean we'd be in slightly better shape for what I was pretty sure was going to be some lively work on the rapids. We'd seen how the rivers were generally high, and far more white than blue, interspersed with plenty of threatening-looking rocks, and I had a feeling we'd be in for another bumpy ride.

The TA was quite a basic one, but it did have a doctor who sprayed my eye, which by now was almost completely closed. But the spray seemed to do the trick and it was a relief to be able to see properly out of my right eye again.

I've always had a soft spot, as it were, for my right eye. Some years ago, in the interests of more efficient adventure racing, I had had my short-sighted eyes treated by laser. (Contact lenses are not really an option when you're sleepless in the jungle for days on end.) The operation on my right eye seemed at first not to have worked; for days I went around less able to see out of it than I had been before. Then on a particularly rough bike ride I'd got whacked in the face by the branch of a low-lying tree. Hard, and bang on my half-blind eye. To my astonishment, I could see clear as a bell after that.

I was glad that, whatever the cause of this new eye injury, it hadn't mysteriously reversed the effect.

The kayaking stage couldn't begin until 5.30 a.m. because we were only allowed on the water in daylight, which was between 5.30 a.m. and 6.30 p.m. Understandable really, considering how dangerous the whole thing was even when it wasn't dark.

We had to trek from the TA carrying all the paddling equipment, and needed to time our arrival at the kayak point for 5.30 on the dot to make the most of our time. So it was annoying that we went the wrong way for four or five kilometres on the trek and ended up having to run in order to be there on time. Even more annoying to discover that two teams were just setting off ahead of us, and the whole process of getting into the water was slowed down by a briefing process.

We were standing on the edge of the river, paddles ready, kit packaged tightly to the boats, and pulling up the red two-seater kayaks to the side of the bank. The river was flowing fast; probably a class 2 rapid, but we were told that it would turn into a class 3 – a faster, more difficult – rapid later on.

'You *will* capsize,' said the official. He seemed to sound more pleased at the thought than concerned for our welfare. 'You have the option of portaging (carrying the boats on land), but be aware that your presence is not always welcome. If you capsize and need help, do not approach the indigenous population. Wait for them to come to you.'

We looked at each other. None of this was particularly encouraging, but mostly we just wanted to get on with it. Get in the water and make some progress after a slightly frustrating start to the day.

The first hour or so was good going, and it was even rather a relief to be sitting down and able to admire the scenery. But soon we realised the race official had a point. We found ourselves being pulled and pushed by the water as the current seemed to flow faster and faster.

Soon the previously quite placid river became a rushing torrent of fast-flowing water with sharp grey rocks sticking out of it. The rocks came at you from every direction, and try as we might it was impossible to keep the boats steady. Karen and Simon were the first to go over, quickly followed by me and Staffan. We were thrown away from the boats and found ourselves hurtling down the river.

Somehow we grabbed the kayaks back, righted them and set off again. There was a big bend in the river, and as we rounded it we saw that we were being joined by another river where the rocks were even bigger and the water even more of a mass of foaming white froth. We managed to hang on for another half an hour, tense with the effort of adjusting the boat to the swirling movement below. And then, no good. The water took our boat and seemed to toss it to one side. Moments later, the same thing happened to Karen and Staffan.

The four of us and the two boats eddied on downstream until we could gather our strength and get back in.

Karen was furious. 'This is not right,' she said as we got everything back together on the side of a bank. 'These are more like class 4 rapids.'

I agreed, but thought it best just to get back in the boats and carry on. But there was such a high chance of crashing, and it was certainly one of the fastest rivers I've ever been expected to race in.

Eventually we found some less lively parts of the river, near the banks, but by now we were going against the current, which made paddling very hard work. But it seemed to be the price we had to pay for not capsizing every twenty minutes.

Carrying the kayaks along the road to the next TA, we decided not to hang about but to just get on our bikes as soon as we could. That next leg was a mere forty-two kilometres, it was daylight, and it was part of our game plan to just keep going. This was the beginning of 'our' stage of the race, the part of the race where we would push on hard while everyone else was getting tired. Maybe we would grab an hour or two of sleep at the next TA, but for now we needed to move on fast.

Grabbing the bikes out of their boxes, I found myself angry again at the state of my bike. The gearbox was looking no better than it had been on the last bike leg, and the chain seemed to be more full of sand than oil. I put lube and oil on it again, and hoped that it wouldn't hold us up on this next vital stage.

Just as worrying was Simon. He seemed to be getting slower on the trek back from the river, and didn't have his usual zest. Normally you have to stop Simon running ahead and expending twice as much energy as a bouncy Tigger, but now I couldn't help noticing that he was moving that little bit more slowly. And, although he is never a great chatter, he wasn't saying very much even for him.

But we didn't have time to spare on any ailments – ours or our machines'. And we set off at speed from the TA, all of us hoping it would get easier to make good progress.

It was a steep section. Nearly all the trails seemed to be up rather than down, although thankfully we were now down nearly at sea level so at least we were able to pant properly.

I was just starting to think that we were making up some good time when Staffan's bike suddenly veered off the track. A puncture. Swearing to myself, I signalled to the others to stop while we investigated the damage. Our bikes were super-expensive and top-of-the-range, but however top-of-the-range, bikes still get punctures and over the years we've repaired them with the crudest tools – once even using a farmer's drill to make the tiny (top-of-the-range) valves bigger so we could use his pump to inflate the tyres.

This time, though, we were able to solve the problem with our own kit. Taking one of our silver blankets and some duct tape, Karen managed to get the blanket to block the hole, and then tape up the tyre and inflate it so we could move on. Staffan's bike looked in a pretty sorry state by the time we'd finished the operation, but at least its wheels went round with him on it.

Once back on the bikes our progress still wasn't as great as it should have been. Simon was definitely at the back at this stage, and although no one said so out loud, I could sense that he was starting to struggle. About ten kilometres from the next TA the going got really steep, and Simon was finding it harder to disguise how difficult he was finding it. He's a very tough athlete who never complains, so he's actually very hard to read.

We were by now in the middle of the Mache-Chindul Ecological Reserve, an area of rainforest that protects the famous Cube Lake – a system of lakes in the middle of wetlands, famous for its varieties of orchids and monkeys. Needless to say, orchids and monkeys weren't on my mind as we struggled up the steep track to TA8.

This transition area was a sports centre in real life, although a fairly basic one. In effect it was just a huge concrete rectangle covered by an open metal roof. It sat at the top of a hill rising out of the village of Y de Cube, a collection of shacks made of wood, breeze blocks and corrugated iron. At one end of the rectangle was a sort of makeshift stage, and all around the edges were groups of athletes surrounded by bike boxes and gearboxes.

There was a hum of activity as people laid out kit to dry and sorted out what they were going to need for the next stage – a trek through the thickest and most remote part of the jungle. So remote that part of it wasn't even mapped; we were going to be allowed GPS navigation to get through that part as it would otherwise have been impossible.

The organisers had warned us that this stretch of the race was the hardest – impenetrable, pathless and full of flying, biting creatures. The going, we were told, would be bad to terrible. The ground would mostly be a series of muddy bog holes that would suck you in completely at worst, or slow you down to crawling pace at best. Then the racebook cheerfully informed us that 'in spite of the difficulty, the jungle is beautiful'.

I had half thought we might catch up on an hour's sleep at the next stage, but looking around at the team now I thought we might need a bit more than that.

I could sense that Karen was getting impatient – sometimes, being so strong herself, she doesn't always understand other people's weakness. But whatever else was true, I knew we all needed to focus on getting some rest. We had had maybe five hours' sleep in five days, and I knew that we didn't have the strength to race this next bit at our best if we didn't pause at least for an hour or two.

Knowing that the others were feeling the pain made me feel somehow stronger. I realised that it was like when I was in the military: when other people run out of strength, I seem to get stronger. I think suffering is a skill I have.

I laid out my kit, putting everything on the ground item by item – throughout my career I'd never lost or forgotten anything, and I wasn't about to start now. I put my battered and bruised bike away with some relief. We all worked silently, cleaning what we could and putting on fresh shirts and socks. Of course they were only going to be immersed in mud, but changing clothes was still important if only to try to stop the dirt and damp building up.

The next leg was such a tough one that we decided we would have an extra dose of protein and carbohydrate, so I warmed up two packs of meatballs with pasta. They came with their own thermal sleeve, so you could generate heat around the packs and end up with something almost like a proper meal. These packs are the equivalent of a five-star dinner in the world of adventure racing.

As we sat down to get the food ready, I noticed out of the corner of my eye an unmoving figure by a pile of bike boxes a few yards away. As a TA is usually a mass of moving parts – people rushing to change, to pack, to unpack – such a still silhouette caught my eye.

It was a muddy, battered-looking dog. He was standing perfectly still by a red bike box. He seemed to be waiting for something. People were milling around him, but he looked completely unperturbed by all the activity just inches away from him.

I had seen lots of stray dogs in Ecuador, but had never taken much notice of them. Mostly they were sad-looking creatures, with injured legs and missing ears. They would yap and bite and jump about, or they'd howl, or they'd just collapse in a heap asleep. But I had never seen a dog with such presence, such stillness.

He was big, and underneath the mud and dirt I thought he was probably a golden colour. Even at a distance I could see that some of the mud was blood; he had bad wounds as well as dirt on him.

But he was so stoical, so dignified, he caught my eye by his very appearance of calm. As I watched, he turned in my direction and padded forwards a few paces. I could see now that he was looking at me.

Still a few yards away, he wasn't making any kind of fuss; he was just looking. I glanced around at the others. They were focused on their food, on their kit.

I looked back at the dog. 'You're in a mess, my friend,' I thought. 'You're not complaining, but you're in a bad way.'

He was looking at me unblinkingly.

I knew nothing about dogs. Never had one, never wanted one, but I could see that this dog was somehow special. It was as if he had some sort of inner calm, as if he knew stuff.

I opened the pack of meatballs. They were now warmed and looked meaty and good. I put a spoon into the mass inside, got up and moved towards the dog.

He carried on looking at me as I approached. Neither coming nearer nor moving away, just looking at me. I got a little nearer, and I bent down and put a spoonful of the meatballs on the ground in front of him. I decided that one wasn't enough and added another one to the pile of meat in front of the dog.

'There you go,' I said.

Finally he stopped looking at me and, bending his big head down to the ground, he wolfed the lot almost in one go. 'You were hungry, my friend,' I said to him under my breath.

As a boy, I dreamt of being a professional ice hockey player, and was devastated when I didn't make the cut.

But things took a turn for the better when I met Helena when I was just seventeen.

Team Peak Performance at the Adventure World Championship. We knew it would be hard, but we didn't know the emotional journey that was about to unfold.

At first, Arthur was just this scruffy dog who wandered over for meatballs. I thought he was only interested in me for food.

I can't say why, but Arthur just seemed so relaxed around me, and I was relaxed around him. Though it helped that I was exhausted.

There was just something about him. I knew nothing about dogs, yet I felt straight away that we understood each other.

Arthur sleeping. Perhaps he knew he had a long road ahead.

When we got to the kayaking segment, I knew the sensible thing was to leave Arthur behind. But Arthur had different ideas, and jumped in the water behind us.

Arthur wasn't a strong swimmer, and I had to pull him into the boat with us.

The race was tough for all of us, and we were so worried about Arthur's injuries and health. But he wouldn't leave us, and he just became part of the team.

Arthur was a pro at kayaking by now.

I think here Arthur has decided he is team captain!

By the time we got to the finish, I knew I couldn't leave Arthur. We may have lost the race, but I had found a best friend.

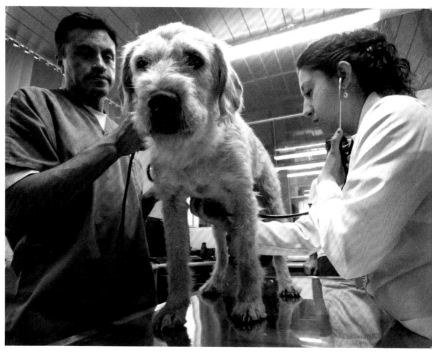

In Quito, we had to take Arthur to the vet's. He had a severe injury on his back and problems with his teeth.

Despite the pain he must have been in, Arthur was always so friendly. Here he is thanking the vets for their help.

When we went to the airport to fly Arthur back to Sweden, there were hundreds of reporters there.

The beginning of Arthur's celebrity. You can see the wounds on his back.

I hated the idea of Arthur having to go into a crate to fly, but it was what we had to do to bring him home.

We arrived in Sweden, where Arthur met Philippa for the first time. But our journey wasn't over yet, as Arthur had to go straight into quarantine.

Leaving him behind was one of the hardest things I have ever had to do.

Closer up I could see that a lot of the mud was indeed dried blood and he had wounds all over him. And when he looked back up at me, every last drop of gravy eaten, I could see that his ears were in a bad way too. I could smell him, too. It wasn't a good smell. 'Wow,' I thought, 'you have not had an easy time of it, have you? You probably have all the diseases I've ever heard of. Rabies, the lot.'

Then I thought how tough it must be to be a stray dog in this country, dependent on the kindness of strangers. Because some of the natives sure don't show much kindness. I'd seen enough of them kicking and throwing stones at passing dogs to know that this was not a place where people were always brought up to treat animals kindly. I hoped this dog would be OK.

I turned away from him and went back to the others. It was getting dark, and Simon was making slow progress with his kit, so I went over to help him get organised. I then finished packing every bit of my own stuff, carefully piling the layers into my backpack and doing up the buckles. The others were getting ready to lie down and rest.

'Twenty minutes,' I said to my teammates. 'And then we've got our biggest test of all.'

Chapter 6

'Are You Coming With Us?'

'The first rule of adventure racing is that anything can happen. Sometimes the most unexpected things.'

Only moments later, or so it seemed, and everyone was up and getting ready to move off. The TA was a mass of people, all seemingly going in different directions. It was dark by now, so with headlamps and kit on, we took a moment to double-check the map – not an easy job, as our lights seemed to attract every passing saucer-sized moth in the jungle. I reckoned we were some hours behind the leaders, but with luck and a good push we could make up some time on this section. There was everything to play for.

Simon was slow getting to his feet, and so was Staffan. I knew we all really wanted more sleep.

'Hey, we can do this,' I said. 'We can make good time here. Come on, let's go now.'

I had seen that two teams, including our old friends the Swedish Armed Forces, had just left the TA. If we got going immediately we could catch them up, I thought.

I led my team out of the camp, feeling really good and moving quickly. Perhaps my energy infected the others as it was meant to, because soon we were hard on the heels of the other Swedish team.

Once we caught up with them, we started chatting as we walked. I like talking to other racers, partly because I like the banter, partly because sometimes you can find out their weak spots and store up the information for future use. I've often got our team in the lead by knowing other people's weaknesses or playing mind games. (It's amazing how you can remind people of their injuries by asking them about them just before a race. It's like sledging in cricket; we all do it.)

On this occasion, even though I knew we were very little restored by twenty minutes' sleep, and that we had a lot of work to do on this section, I behaved as if I didn't have a care in the world and we all had limitless energy.

We were all talking about how the race organisers had given us a list of the huge range of rare animals we might see on this leg – ocelots, raccoons, pumas, jaguars, alligators, snapping turtles. And snakes, lots of snakes – they had even marked the area 'Snake Zone' in the race's roadbook.

I was ahead of everyone else and nearly trod on what I thought was the root of a tree in the middle of the path. It was only as I glanced back at it that I saw it move in a rather sinister way. 'There's one,' I called out cheerfully to a Swedish guy who I knew had a bit of a snake phobia. 'Definitely venomous,' I added.

He looked rather perturbed. Part of me thought of saying to him, Well you are in the snake zone, what do you expect? And the other part thought, This could gain us some time if they have to stop and look after a team member who's freaking out.

Then I heard one of the others at the back of the group shout out to our team who were in front, 'Hey, you bringing a dog with you?'

I looked back and for a moment couldn't see anything except hundreds of giant insects dancing in the blaze of everyone's headlamps. Then I made out a shape in the darkness at the back. I was concentrating on moving forwards as fast as possible, and I couldn't really see what it was, so I gave a shrug and turned back to focus on the track ahead of us.

We carried on at a pretty fast pace for a bit, and then amazingly I saw another snake right in the middle of the path. This one was dressed in bright yellow, orange and black. From somewhere deep in my memory came a child-hood rhyme:

Red Touch Yellow – Kills a Fellow
Red Touch Black – Venom Lack
Yellow Touches Red – Soon You'll Be Dead
Red Touches Black – Friend of Jack

'Yellow touches red, that one,' I said. 'Soon you'll be dead,' I added for good measure, laughing.

'Not funny,' said Mr Snake Phobia, panic in his voice. 'No, that is not funny.'

'Or maybe it's red touches yellow. You can't quite see. Anyway – kills a fellow,' I went on.

'That is not funny. No way. That is not funny.' Mr Snake Phobia stopped and his teammates all stopped too and surrounded him.

I marched on ahead, fast, the others managing to keep up. We set up a very good pace and soon we had left the others behind and were on an uphill track lead-ing towards the part of the jungle for which we had no map.

Simon was making good progress, although I could tell he was digging deep in his own bucket of pain. But now Staffan was slowing.

'Staffan?' I said from the front. 'How you doing?'

'Not good,' he said. 'Knee's bad. Plus I could do with a kip.' He sounded so sleepy as he spoke.

'I'll take your pack,' I said. I seemed to be feeling stronger and stronger, and anyway, this was kind of a payback for him towing me on the bikes earlier in the race. We stopped for me to take his pack.

And that's when I saw the shape that had been following us draw near. It was the dog that I had given the meatballs to. He must have come after us as soon as we left the TA; he'd been following us, then, not the other team.

'Hey,' said Karen, 'Isn't that the dog you gave the food to?'

'Yes,' I said. 'He was hungry. I guess he still is. But I expect he'll go back home soon.'

We turned round and set off again. We were still making good progress, and I still felt good even though I was carrying two backpacks. Then the track started to get muddier. And muddier. I decided we would have a pause to fix our boots and our backpacks. This next bit was going to be very hard going, so we needed to have our kit and our boots tightly buckled and bound.

There was no sign of any team behind us, so we took a moment to sit on some stones by the side of the trail. Our lamps created a pool of light in front of us as we worked on fixing our feet.

Aware of a movement by my side, I looked up. It was the dog. He was just standing there, quite still, looking ahead onto the track.

'Hey, doggie,' I said. 'Shouldn't you be going home?'

The dog turned his head and looked up at me briefly and then looked back at the track ahead. It suddenly crossed my mind that perhaps he didn't have a home.

I bent down a bit so I could see into his face. He was surveying the scene through half-shut eyes. As I got closer he looked all around him, everywhere but at me. Almost as if he were embarrassed by my close inspection.

'What's going on, doggie?' I said. 'Are you going to come with us?'

Then he looked up at me again, looked me full in the eye. And by the light of my headlamp I could see his eyes were amber, and he had a dark line round them.

But I could also see, now that my light was shining on his back, just how terrible his wounds looked. His fur was matted and black. I thought again of the disease and infections he probably carried around with him.

As if reading my thoughts, he looked up at me again, then blinked and looked away. With one smooth movement, he lay down flat in front of me. He put his head down on his paws as if settling in for a bit of a sleep.

'What's your plan, fella?' I said to him, bending down to him. 'We're going deep into the jungle. It's going to be tough.'

The dog looked up at me again. I could hear the others getting to their feet, and I started to get up myself. I looked over at Staffan for a moment, and when I looked back at the dog he was back on his feet and looking up at me.

'You sure about this?' I said to him softly.

'Hey.' Staffan was on the other side of the track, bending over as if in pain. 'We're nearly at the GPS stage. I'm not sure I'm up to navigating.'

I stood up, now fully focused on the job in hand. Staffan was – is – our chief navigator. He has saved us so many hours in so many races by his skilled route-finding and cunning navigation.

But I looked at him now, and I could see that he was not in good shape. I knew that one thing that would help with the pain of his knee would be proper stretching. When you're that far gone you can't do it yourself; you need someone pretty brutal to stretch your muscles for you.

He knew the drill, and lay down on his side. I took his leg and stretched it, forwards and sideways. He groaned a little, and lay there a little longer, but it seemed to have helped a bit.

'Thanks,' he said. 'Still can't do the GPS though.'

'It's fine,' said Karen. 'I'll do it.' Staffan handed over the GPS and we looked again at the last bit of map, so we could at least get our route into the jungle right.

We passed through a last village before we hit the remote, difficult bit. It was a typical bunch of breeze-block houses, and full of what I now realised were typical bunches of stray dogs. As I looked at a group of them in a corner by a pile of rubbish I thought what a brutal time they must have of it.

We were having one last look at the map, and as we were standing there, with the dog next to us, some of the strays came up to us. They started jumping up and yapping at the dog. But he didn't respond, he just stood there in the midst of the chaos and yowling, looking around him as if nothing was happening. He seemed like the only grown-up, the only dog with dignity and manners.

As we moved on, I was aware that all the time Simon was getting quieter and quieter. He almost seemed to be moving as if sheer willpower alone was pushing him forward.

'Come on,' I said, 'let's hit this bit of trail. We can still make good time here.'

We set off again, me in the lead next to Karen, who had the GPS in her hand ready to go. We were managing a good pace, and the going had got a bit easier.

I looked down to my left. The dog was walking almost exactly in step with me. It was as if there were an invisible lead connecting us. We were still climbing, and the going was still OK. I thought to myself that I didn't know why they kept saying this stretch was so hard; it seemed pretty good to me. If only we could all summon up a bit more energy then we would be in a good position.

But an hour later and I started to understand why this was called the hard bit. We were on the GPS stretch and in proper jungle forest and proper deep mud.

I looked down at our stray by my side.

'Come on, doggie,' I said to him.

He looked up at me when he heard my voice. 'This is your country,' I said. 'Why don't you show us the way?'

I stepped back a bit, so that he was a bit in front of me. He seemed to understand what his job was, and padded ahead towards a bit of jungle that looked completely impenetrable and didn't seem to have any path at all.

We followed him into the densest part. He walked confidently forward; he knew where he was going. But as we shone our lights around the area – through the thick clouds of flying insects – there didn't seem to be any paths anywhere. The general direction of the GPS route was across the jungle and towards the sea. It was just a question of finding our way around the forest and the contour lines on the way.

To start with, following our jungle friend seemed to make sense. We were matching the GPS route, and I found myself literally stepping into the paw-prints the dog made as he walked ahead of us.

'He knows where we're going,' I shouted to the others behind me, pleased that our new guide seemed to know the jungle so well. I followed him round the next bend in the vegetation, smiling to myself. I reckoned there weren't any other racers making use of Ecuador's resources like we were right now.

We carried on tramping through the mud for another hour, in silence except for the howler monkeys who screamed and shouted at us as we got deeper and deeper into the vegetation. Then we came to a clearing that looked a little bit familiar.

'Aieeee,' I said, sounding like a howler monkey myself.

'That's a circle we've just completed. Let's see now, how's the GPS looking?'

We didn't seem to be too far out, but we needed to go downhill more. I had to admit that our jungle friend probably didn't know where we were going any more than we did.

But at this point we could just about pick out something that looked like a track. It was thick, thick mud. I said to everyone that we should take it fast, really run down it. That way we would have the advantage of the downhill, and be able to jump from mud hole to mud hole.

I set off. And I ran down the hill, jumping on the edges of the mud holes and then leaping on to the next one before the mud could collapse and suck me in. I felt exhilarated. It was working. I carried on for another hundred metres, hoping that my example would inspire the others to follow – literally – in my footsteps.

I came to the bottom of the run and a fork in the trail. I looked back. The dog was trotting alongside the edge of the path just a few metres behind me; he'd managed to find a bit of the path where his paws didn't sink right into the mud – but the others were further back, with Simon at the rear.

As they caught up with me, I decided we should check our route. The vegetation was getting thicker, beside us, under us and over us. The insects were dancing about in the lights as much as ever, and if you stood still you sank into the mud up to your knees.

'OK,' said Karen, bending over the GPS and making it zoom in. 'We're here, the fork's here. We go left.'

'Right, everyone,' I said. 'Let's go. The faster the better, that way we won't sink.'

I set off down the left fork. I could tell that the dog was trying to match me step for step, but sometimes one of his paws would sink deep into the mud and he'd have to slow right down. Looking neither to right nor left, but just straight ahead at the route I was taking, it was as if – like me – he was using all his willpower just to put one paw in front of the other.

The others were following as fast as they could, but I could see that none of them were up to using speed to get through the mud quickly. I thought myself back on the Russian border with a troopload of marines behind me. Don't tell, show, I said to myself: if I go fast and hard then they will too. The howler monkeys were making more noise than ever now, almost as if they were laughing at us.

After about an hour of painfully slow progress, I started to have a bad feeling. I waited for the others. 'Let me see the GPS,' I said to Karen. I looked hard at it; Staffan looked hard at it. I could see that for all our efforts we had gone hardly any distance at all.

I also saw that we should have taken the right fork. The howler monkeys really were laughing at us.

I swore. Loudly and long. And then I realised that we needed to go back up the other way, back into the deepest part of the jungle.

Staffan seemed to be moving a little bit better. But Simon was now absolutely silent. I could tell he was putting all his energy into just walking.

'OK Simon?' I said. He nodded. He was moving well, but I could tell it was hard work for him. The sooner we were all back on the right track the better, I thought. So I led the way up the route that seemed to go up and out towards the west and the coast and the direction of the next TA.

For another two hours we trudged up the trail. As we were now walking uphill, it was almost impossible for our legs not to be sucked in by the thick, viscous mud, so we had to expend huge amounts of energy that we couldn't afford just to put one foot in front of the other.

'It's like walking with dumb-bells on your feet, isn't it?' said Karen. Even she was feeling the hurt. As she said, sometimes your shoes came out of the mud with your feet, sometimes they didn't. The dog was by my side all the time. Even when he had to stop to pull himself out of a hole, he seemed to make up the time and catch up with us. It was as if he wasn't going to let himself be further than a couple of metres away from me.

Eventually we saw what looked like the edge of the forest at a summit up ahead. It was still dark but we could see that we had emerged into a kind of clearing; we saw grass and different kinds of trees from the forest trees of before.

My bad feeling came back. 'This is no good,' I said. 'There's no way this is right.' I looked again at the GPS. 'We need to go down here, along this line,' I said.

There is no such thing as the wisdom of hindsight on an adventure race. You just take what wisdom you can get. And of course we wouldn't have made those terrible route decisions if we knew then what we found out later. All the time we were trekking, we were of course being followed inch by inch on the computer screens by Helena and the team back home. And they had been holding their breath for the past three hours, because not only were we walking in completely the wrong direction but, in the dark, we were also literally three metres away from the edge of a sheer twenty-metre cliff edge.

Knowing none of this, we scrambled our way to a trail heading downhill, unaware that if we went a few footsteps to the left we would have been permanently out of the race. The downhill was very steep, so it wasn't any easier than going uphill, and we couldn't have run through the mud holes, even if we had had the energy.

I was still feeling pretty good, perhaps just because everything was getting so hard and that's how I am, but all the time I knew that we were all struggling more and more. Simon was now trailing behind, and though Karen and Staffan were determined and still strong enough, I was starting to be aware that the fifth member of our team was really struggling too.

I looked back at him. The mud was dragging him down at every step. Whereas before he'd seemed to have the energy to move his paws quickly enough not to get sucked in, as I watched his progress I could tell that his energy levels had dropped dramatically and he was fighting hard to make any progress at all. I found myself hoping we would get to easier ground soon, so he wouldn't get so tired. But whatever happened we would help him through; he was one of us now.

We had lost a lot of ground in the last six or seven hours. If we were to make up any time we needed to get back on the right trail pretty quickly. For once, my internal prayers seemed to be answered, and as we got to the end of the steep hill we could see clearly how the trail ahead matched the GPS. At last we were back on the right route. As if to echo my hopeful thoughts, the sun started to come up and lit our way as we trekked down through this less dense bit of forest.

The sight of a small river crossing the trail up ahead was a relief. First it confirmed we were on the right track, and second it gave our feet a welcome cooling. It was good to walk through the chill water.

I looked back at the team as I got to the other side. Simon was still moving well, but now seemed to be finding it harder to pretend it was anything like easy. I began to think that this wasn't just the toughness of the race but that maybe there was something wrong as well, like he was sick but pretending not to be.

Behind him I could see the dog. Crouched low over the water, he was lapping fast and loud as if his life depended on it. Which I suppose in some ways it probably did. I watched him as he seemed to hoover up half the river, half pleased that he was able to quench his thirst, half fascinated by the confident, energetic slurping noises.

'Come on.' It was Karen, already ahead and halfway down the next bit of trail. I waited a moment longer to make sure the dog had seen which way we were going. And then as he trotted up to me I realised that I was crazy to think he'd let himself lose sight of us.

The ground was firmer here and soon he was back to walking next to me, at a better pace. We'd only been going another half an hour when suddenly the dog stopped and stood stock-still. I looked down at him. He was completely focused on something in the distance. Looking where he was looking, I could see some animals in a clearing. They looked like wild horses. The dog put his nose in the air, and to my amazement shot off into the jungle.

Right, I thought. That drink at the river's given him extra energy; and now he's seen something he has to chase. Maybe that's the last we'll see of him.

I walked on for a few more minutes, subconsciously looking to my left every now and then to see if the dog had come back. The more minutes that passed the more I convinced myself he wasn't coming back; he'd gone now, he'd found something more interesting than us. I couldn't believe how low that made me feel.

Then I heard a rustle from the undergrowth. I looked round and there he was, trotting up to my side and following in my footsteps just as if nothing had happened. I smiled to myself. I guess sometimes a dog has to do what a dog has to do.

An hour later we'd crossed two more rivers and were

now definitely back on the right route. I decided that we needed a break to sit down and refuel, and try to recharge. The sun was nearly up, so we could see what we were walking on – thick vegetation, thick mud, and possibly the odd snake, but so long as you didn't know that, you didn't have to worry about it.

Through all of this the dog kept up with us. I had now got completely used to his presence by my side, despite his little moment of running off. This battered, mud-spattered creature who – mostly – kept pace with my every stride. I told myself it would be better if he went home, but when he lagged behind, I knew I subconsciously slowed down to wait for him.

Crazy. Every minute counted. But there I was waiting for a dog to catch me up.

We got to a clearing in the jungle. Not a big clearing, just a couple of logs and a bit of flat earth in between them.

'Here,' I said, turning round to the others. 'Let's refocus. Let's see what we've got to eat, let's break.'

One by one we collapsed on the logs. Me and Simon on one, opposite Karen and Staffan on the other. The dog was right by my feet as we sat down. When he saw that we were all sitting, he looked up at me and collapsed himself too. As he put his head down on the ground I could see how truly exhausted he was and how glad he was to be able to stop.

'OK, guys,' I said. 'What have we got? Energy bars? What?'

'Not much,' said Staffan. 'A bar or two, but we'll need those later.'

'Yeah,' said Karen, 'Here's another one, but we've a long way to go, I reckon we'll need them later as well.'

'But look at this.' Simon was scrabbling around in his pack. 'Hey guys, how great is this?' Suddenly he seemed a bit more energetic as he waved not one, but two of our meatball packs in his hand, our five-star adventure racing dinner.

We only had one heating-up thermal collar, so we put them both in it. It was such a bonus to have so many useful calories, so unexpectedly and at exactly the moment we needed them.

Soon the packs were warmed up. Simon handed me the first one. I opened it up and took a mouthful, and passed it back to Simon. He took a bite too, and then there was a pause.

By the side of our clearing was a silent presence. The dog, now more muddy and dirty than ever, was lying quietly by my side. With his big head resting on his paw, he seemed to be waiting patiently for something, anything, or nothing.

As I looked at him, I found myself wondering what had happened to him before he met us, wondering how he had survived, how he'd found anything to eat. *What would he do when he went home?* I thought.

Then Karen said, 'I think he's hungry.'

I looked up. I felt like I'd been jolted out of uncon-sciousness. Yes, I thought, of course he's hungry.

'Yes,' said Staffan, looking at the dog. 'I reckon he hasn't had any proper food since way before you gave him some at the TA.'

'What do you think?' said Karen. 'He needs it more than we do.'

I looked back at the dog. He was lying there quietly, as if the only thing in his world that mattered was to be there sitting on the ground by my side. He must have smelt food, he must have been aware that we were sitting about and going to eat something. But he didn't fuss. He didn't beg. He just lay there quietly, every now and then looking up, just to make sure we were still there.

I looked down at him again. He couldn't be thirsty, not after he'd gulped half the river so noisily. And it was unlikely he was expected back home anywhere anytime soon for his tea. I began to think that maybe he was on his own, and maybe he was in exactly as much trouble as I thought he was in when I first saw him.

'Yes?' Karen's voice interrupted me.

'Yes,' I said. 'This fella's nearly had it. But we can help him. What do you think, everyone?'

My team, my mates, all nodded.

I stood up and, in the midst of all the worry about our time, about our route, I thought for a moment about what a real team decision is. It might be which route to take, when to sleep, when to carry or be carried – but sometimes it's a completely different sort of team decision.

This was ours, I thought, as I got up and went into the jungle. Our decision was: give to somebody something that they needed more than we did.

I wanted to find the right way to say this, the right way to show this dog that we were going to make a fuss of him. I wanted to say to him: we will support you, not everyone is going to cut you and beat you, whatever has happened to you so far, you're going to have some kindness happen to you.

Not saying anything to the others, I went off into the undergrowth. I knew what I was looking for; it was mad, but I knew what I wanted. I wanted to find something that showed that I meant it.

And then, there it was. A huge, exotic leaf. Like the kind of plate you might find at a banquet. I looked down at the leaf and I thought: this is for a banquet fit for a king.

And then I thought about the dog that I had started to think of as a friend. I thought about the way he'd first looked at me. The way he'd sought me out. But I also thought about the way he carried himself, his *pondus*, that Swedish word that conveys so much and which defined his stillness and elegance. He was, he is, like a king. A golden king. Like the film. Like King Arthur. This dog was no ordinary dog. He was regal. He was Arthur.

I walked back to the clearing with my leaf, and I put it on another log. 'OK,' I said to Simon and the others, 'this is for Arthur.'

As we pushed the meatballs out of the packs and on to my banquet leaf, everyone agreed that the name 'Arthur' was right. Kingly, calm, special.

I knew we were all exhausted, all hungry, all trying to win. But as I watched Arthur hoover up our only supplies, I thought, I will look after you.

Whatever it takes.

Chapter 7

Whatever it Takes

'I'm the guy that never quits'

We watched Arthur finish every last drop of gravy, every last trace of meatball. Even when he had definitely and certainly licked the leaf clean he carried on licking. He had had a huge amount of food – maybe 1,200 calories – but it looked like he could eat it all over again.

'You were so hungry, weren't you, Arthur?' I said to him.

I heard a groan on my right. Simon.

'Simon?' I said. 'What's going on?'

'Foot,' he said. 'It's the crack again.' I knew that Simon had gone to the doctor in the past with a cracked foot, from all the running on hard ground and daily training. I guess after five days' racing all our aches and breaks were starting to show.

He looked up at me. He looked almost feverish. There was still a long way to go, nearly all of it through the ferociously sticky mud, and I began to worry that Simon really was sick.

We all stood up, Arthur too, and set off again. At least this time we knew where we were going. The mud was as thick as ever. After about half an hour I looked back at Simon, who had fallen behind. He was walking on, as if trying to pretend nothing was the matter, but I began to worry that he had a case of dehydration.

We had half a water bottle left between us. We stopped and gave the water, a few drops at a time, to Simon.

For a little while after that he seemed better, and we were able to carry on making our slow and painful progress through the jungle. I could see from the GPS that the tenths of a kilometre were ticking down insanely slowly.

Then I heard a groan from Simon. He looked really feverish now and seemed to be moving forward just through sheer force of will. I was now seriously worried. We were a long way from help, we had no water left, and Simon was definitely suffering from dehydration and his injury.

'Come on,' I said. 'Put your arm round me.'

He was reluctant, and tried assuring us he was fine, but I insisted. Looking after each other is what teammates are for, I told him firmly as I brought his left arm up over my shoulder. We lasted this way for another half an hour or so, and then had to pause again by the side of the track.

'Staffan,' I said to him. 'I think we've got to do this together.' Simon was struggling heroically to walk on his own, but if you're suffering from chronic dehydration you need more than willpower and fitness to get you through. So together Staffan and I pulled him up, and with his arms draped round us we staggered on for the next bit of the trek.

I looked down at Arthur as he, too, was struggling through the thick mud. I couldn't help thinking that if Simon hadn't given Arthur his share of the meatballs he, Simon, might be in better shape. But then I looked at Arthur and thought, he's only just with us as it is, even after all that food.

About an hour later we heard a group of athletes approaching from behind. They were one of the 'short course' teams, teams that don't have the full time restrictions of the race and have a short cut to the end. They were Ecuadorians and they looked unbelievably fresh to our eyes as they waded quickly and decisively through the mud towards us.

When they caught up with us they stopped. They looked at Simon and obviously realised how bad he was. The captain of the team asked us in English, 'We'll help you, yes?'

I nodded, not knowing quite what they could do.

The captain then took off his backpack and got out a bottle of energy drink. 'Here,' he said to me. 'You have this for him.'

It was not the first time that a fellow racer has been so generous – I was once about to pass out from dehydration in the Utah desert in temperatures of fifty-five degrees. When the captain of a rival team, Richard Ussher, caught up with us, he gave us the only water he had left. 'Here, have that,' he had said. It was a wonderful moment of sportsmanship, and so was this.

Very slowly and gradually we gave Simon the liquid. He seemed to get a little calmer afterwards, and we were able to carry on towing him through the mud; Karen in front, us three behind, all, by this stage, struggling. We could see glimpses of the coastline through the trees; the next TA wasn't too far now.

Finally, we emerged out of the thick vegetation of the jungle. Blinking in the light, we could see some ramshackle houses and another river ahead of us.

Slowly we edged nearer to the river, past the houses. My one thought was to get Simon in the water, to cool him down. A few metres further down the river was a woman with a huge pile of clothes; she was slapping them on the rocks, shaking them and wringing them out.

Staffan and I headed towards the riverbank. The woman looked round at us, and seemed to be saying something.

'No,' said Karen firmly as we edged towards the side of the water. 'She'll go crazy, you're going to upset her washing if you make the river muddy.'

I looked at her, amazed. Here was Simon in a bad way and we were supposed to worry about someone's washing? But OK, I thought, and we edged Simon a few metres further up the riverbank and then started to walk into the water, with Arthur following us.

Staffan and I used our hands to pour water over Simon, not to drink, just to cool. He grinned and seemed to feel some kind of benefit. We got him back to the bank and looked at the map, to the accompaniment of the now familiar noise of Arthur drinking.

'The TA's just down there,' said Staffan. 'But we need to cross this river. How do we do that?'

'Well, she's got a canoe,' I said, looking at the woman doing her washing. 'We could ask her to row us there.'

Karen looked like we must be joking. But it truly did seem to me to be the only way. Slightly hesitantly she went up to the woman, with the three of us and Arthur following behind.

Karen must have told the woman how ill Simon was, because I could see her putting her washing carefully back on the rock and heading over to her canoe – a long, simple boat with just enough room for us four and her.

We walked over towards her and smiled and nodded and smiled and nodded. She seemed happy to help, and we were just happy to be helped. We put Simon in the boat first and managed to lie him down flat, and then one by one got in behind him.

Arthur had now finished drinking, and had followed us to the canoe. As we bent over Simon, Arthur gave a little whimper. And then, when Staffan got into the canoe, he started whimpering even more.

'What shall we do with Arthur?' I said.

'He can swim,' said Staffan. 'I'm sure he can swim.'

But I could see that Arthur was getting more and more distressed as first Karen and then I followed the others into the canoe. Arthur started trotting in agonised circles as the woman picked up her paddle, got into the canoe and pushed us off.

In between trying to nod and smile our thanks to the washerwoman I watched Arthur on the shore. He was now whimpering loudly and his circles were getting bigger and bigger. I looked at him and tried to will him to get in the water and come after us. 'Come on, come on,' I found myself muttering under my breath. 'You can swim, you MUST be able to swim.'

We were now getting further away, and I was just beginning to despair when Arthur suddenly jumped up on to the rock with our kind boatswoman's washing on it. Scrabbling around and nearly slipping off it, he somehow managed to push the whole pile of washing back into the river.

Poor thanks for the great favour she was doing us, but I felt huge elation as he splashed into the water and started swimming after us.

I tried to stay still and calm in the boat, but a lot of me was looking back at Arthur as he struggled after us. He clearly wasn't happy swimming and he was making such slow progress.

'Come on Arthur,' I found myself shouting, 'Come on, you can do it!'

We were now halfway to the landing stage and the last short trek before the next TA. Only another hundred metres to go, and Arthur was still swimming.

'Hey boy,' Karen shouted. 'Nearly there.'

Our washerwoman paddler was making slow progress too – not surprising with one paddle and five people – but soon we were only inches away from the landing stage on the other side of the river.

As we helped pull up the boat and lift Simon out, I was aware that Arthur only had three metres to go. He looked absolutely exhausted; he seemed to scarcely know how to swim, so he was expending vast amounts of energy trying to stay afloat and move forwards. Perhaps if he hadn't had all those meatballs he couldn't have made it.

Finally he got to the bank and emerged from the water beside us, his wet fur making him look thin and bedraggled. We gave a cheer, but it looked as if his legs could scarcely carry him, and as if to prove it he dropped suddenly to the ground.

Our priority was to get Simon to medical help, so Staffan and I pulled Simon's arms around us and, knowing we were so near help and the TA, somehow found extra strength to get through the last bit of muddy trek.

As we struggled up the hill to the TA through some bamboo shoots, with Arthur walking beside us, I heard Krister's voice among the noise of the people waiting by the approach. I guessed he was taking photos, but I couldn't think of anything by this stage except the fact that we had a man in urgent need of medical attention.

As we got nearer to the TA – a crude and basic one this, not much more than a concrete area for our boxes and sleeping mattresses – I found myself shouting 'Medic, here, we need a medic.' Simon was trying to tell us not to fuss, but he couldn't get the words out properly and wasn't very convincing. Three or four people came out of a canvas cabin by the side of the area where all the athletes gathered and came towards us. Staffan and I handed Simon over with great relief and the doctors took him into the medical tent and laid him down on a canvas stretcher that doubled as a hospital bed. By this stage Simon seemed almost incapable of speech, and was just emitting a low groan.

'OK,' said one of the doctors when he'd looked at his eyes and taken his pulse. 'This guy's in a bad way. We can rehydrate him a bit, but really he needs IV.'

Putting a competitor on an intravenous drip meant a four-hour penalty. In theory we could just patch up Simon, put him in the kayaks for the next stage and do all his paddling for him.

But this was more serious than any four-hour penalty, and I didn't want to endanger Simon. So I said, 'Yes, he needs IV. Can you do that now? Can you do that really quickly?' I could see Karen was about to say something, and Staffan was looking the other way. I was captain though, and I'd made my decision.

The medics attached the drip to Simon's arm. He had closed his eyes and as the drip started its work, he seemed to drift off into unconsciousness. There was no more to be done but wait for the rehydration process to finish, and for us to make the best of a four-hour penalty.

I led the others out of the tent, and wasn't a bit surprised to see Arthur standing patiently by the entrance. His close encounter with the river hadn't seemed to make him any less dirty, but then by this stage we were all completely and deeply filthy.

He followed us as Karen, Staffan and I went over to some concrete steps and found our gear. At least we could have a change of footwear for the next stage and get some rest. Arthur watched closely as I peeled off my mud-encrusted socks. Perhaps he wanted to make sure I wasn't going anywhere – or perhaps he just wanted to remind me that he was still there just in case there were some more meatballs going.

As he looked patiently up at me, waiting for some sort of action, a couple of foxlike stray dogs came up to him and started yapping at him. Perhaps they thought he was better at begging and it would be a good idea to latch on to him, or perhaps they thought that he was weakened from all his wounds and they would be able to keep him away from any food that might come his way.

But Arthur, living up to his name, just remained calm and still and regal in his bearing, looking up at me and completely ignoring the noise and nonsense that the two strays were making.

Eventually they gave up and headed off to the other side of the TA, and I got up to see if there were any more meatballs in our boxes of gear. When I found two more packs I decided that this time the three of us should have some. Krister was watching us as we got the meals ready, camera in hand. 'I bet you you'll give yours to the dog,' he said.

And he was right. As I gave Arthur half of my portion of meatballs, I was vaguely aware of clicking noises coming from Krister's camera.

The next stage of the race was the kayak stage. This time it was on safer water so we were allowed to race at night-time, which was just as well because by the time Simon was rehydrated and we'd had our four-hour penalty it would be nearly dark. We also knew that we needed to wait another three hours because then the tide would be up and we could go out with the tide. So by then it would be pitch dark. Given that we had to take this time, we all decided we'd make a virtue of it and get some proper rest.

Arthur followed me as I headed off into a quiet corner of the TA. Or at least a slightly less noisy corner. I lay down on one of our battered mattresses, put an eye shade on, lay completely still and hoped for sleep to overtake me. Exhausted though I was, I remained completely aware of everything that was going on around me, so I heard Krister saying to someone: 'See the dog? He's asleep but he's got one eye open. It's like he's making sure Mikael doesn't go anywhere.'

I smiled inwardly. And found myself drifting off to sleep.

The next thing I knew it was dark and there was action everywhere. Simon was up and rested and he and Karen and Staffan were getting their gear ready for this next leg. The first part was a short trek, and we would have to carry our paddles and boat equipment to get to the kayaks, so there was a lot to get right. We could be on the water for up to fifteen hours non-stop, so we needed to take food and water as well as paddling gear and trekking gear for the walks at each end.

As I focused on packing and repacking and getting everything in the right order, I was aware of Arthur standing just by me the whole time. I hadn't allowed myself to think of what was going to happen to him next. We were going to be kayaking for sixty kilometres through mangrove swamps and through rivers that circled islands and sandbanks.

It couldn't be more absurd or more impossible for us to have a dog in tow.

We set off from the TA, laden down with equipment, and together the five of us walked to the bridge where the boats were ready for the next stage. Even though it was dark there seemed to be quite a lot of people around when we arrived at the organisational point for the beginning of the boat leg.

'You can't bring the dog.'

Even though it was dark, I could see that the race organiser was looking me hard in the eye as he said it. Though I'd known deep down for the last hour that he was going to say this, still as I looked back at him my mind was in turmoil.

Part of me wanted to scream: 'He's not "the dog", he's Arthur. He needs me, I'm his only hope.' Another part of me, looking around at the concerned expressions on everyone's faces, knew that it was crazy, insane, mad, to be thinking about a stray dog when there was so much at stake for us.

We were headed for at least fourteen hours of kayaking, often through difficult waters. Simon had only just recovered from severe dehydration. We would need all our resources to pull ourselves through this next stage. The last thing we should hamper ourselves with was a wounded, sick and exhausted dog. Kayaking would be tough enough with all the changes of tide and the sand-banks blocking our routes.

I looked at Karen, who looked like what she was: one of the toughest athletes in the world. She looked utterly focused on the gear for this next stage of the race. It was hard to remember that this was the same person who gave her share of our last bag of food to a hungry dog in the jungle.

Staffan, too, was eyeing up his kit, already – I knew – mentally in the boat and planning his routes down the rapids. Simon, toughing it out, and obviously determined to get back in the race, just looked at me, waiting for my decision.

And then I looked down. The terrible wound in the middle of Arthur's back seemed if anything to have got darker and bigger. Caked in mud, and trembling slightly, Arthur was in a bad way. But his gaze was firm and strong as he looked up at me unwaveringly and trustingly.

We were now a long, long way from where we had first met him. Wherever home was, even if he had had one, he probably wouldn't have the strength to get back to it now. It was as if Arthur had put everything on one ticket. Me.

I seemed to be looking at him for ever. I must have forgotten to blink, because I could feel a pricking in my eyes. I knew for certain that it was dangerous as well as damaging to us to consider taking him any further. Miles and miles back we had tried to tell him to go home for his own good. But Arthur had steadfastly ignored all our gesticulations and encouragements. Whatever happened, he was determined to come with us.

I bent down to him and put my hand on his head. 'What shall we do, my friend?' I said to him under my breath. 'What shall we do?'

Arthur started to whimper, just a little whimper to start with, and then when I couldn't say anything more, he started to give a little whine in between the whimpers. I put my head nearer to his and said again, 'What shall we do? I don't know, I don't know.'

I felt sick, as if I were contemplating the greatest betrayal of my life. I looked at the others, and the race organisers.

I swallowed hard and stood up. 'I understand,' I said. 'Of course. I understand. He'll find his way back somehow. He will. Dogs are clever like that, aren't they?' I looked around at the staring faces, desperate for reassurance. One by one they nodded, but none of them quite met my eye.

'We must go,' said Staffan. 'The tide's right, and we can have a good start if we get going straight away.'

We gathered up our paddles and our packs, and started to walk towards the bridge where the kayaks were waiting for us.

On the way we passed Krister's van. I knew there was some kit in there. Things for him and his guide to sleep on if they got stuck somewhere. Without thinking, I opened the back door. I knew there were some sheets of plastic and a thin mattress inside. I grabbed a sheet of plastic, and tore off the material from half of one of the mattresses.

I didn't look at anybody. I didn't say anything. There wasn't anything *to* say. I walked with the others to the boats, hardly aware of putting one foot in front of the other. I knew Arthur was following us, but I couldn't look back. I kept telling myself he'd realise what was happening, and that he'd have to stay behind. It was hopeless. I'd never see him again.

But still I clutched the mattress close to me.

One by one we got into the kayaks. Karen and Staffan in the first boat, me and Simon in the second one. I shoved my kit and the plastic and the bit of mattress in the bottom of the boat.

Simon was in front and getting ready to paddle as we pushed off. By now there were lots more people on the bridge and on the bank. We could hear a murmur of voices as we balanced ourselves in the kayak. I told myself not to look back. There was no point. Must not look back.

As I gave a strong pull on the paddle, I felt a hard knot in my stomach. I could hardly see the water beside me; I could hardly see anything.

Then I heard a splash.

There was a gasp from the crowd standing on the bridge. I could hear more murmurings. Subconsciously, I rearranged the plastic on my legs and the mattress flat on the bottom of the boat. Still I pulled hard on the paddle, keeping time with Simon in front of me.

We were starting to lose ground to the others in front. I knew we weren't going nearly as quickly as we should be and that we would lose yet more valuable time if we didn't increase our pace. But still, even as I pushed hard against the resistance of the water, every inch of me was listening for what was happening behind.

There was another splash. I looked round. Arthur, his big head only just above the waterline, was only a few feet behind us, paddling as fast as he could. I knew the water was nearly freezing, and I knew from seeing him in the river the day before that Arthur wasn't a good swimmer. But still, he was now only a couple of feet behind the boat.

When I pulled once more on my paddle, our boat drew away again, further ahead of Arthur. As I looked back at him he seemed to put in another ferocious effort to speed up.

Karen and Staffan's boat was now much further ahead.

I gave another pull on the paddle and we made up a bit more ground on them. I turned back to see that Arthur had fallen further behind. His paws were moving more slowly now, and his head was a little deeper in the water. But as the water churned about us, I could see that still he was looking at me with an unwavering stare.

I found myself talking to myself, in the way that I usually only do if I'm in real danger. This is it, I told myself, this is it. If you do this, it's for good. No matter how damaged he is, how sick, he will be yours and your responsibility. You can't ever push him away from you. You must love him. You and he will be together for ever if you do this. It's for good.

'Stop, Simon,' I said. Simon stopped and looked round.

We slowed down. Once Arthur could see that he was getting nearer, he seemed to find strength from somewhere and, with a supreme effort, got to the side of the boat.

Putting my paddle down, I leaned over and put my hands into the water and around Arthur. With a huge effort, nearly unbalancing the boat as I did so, I pulled him up into the boat.

Chapter 8
Swim for Life

*'He's in a bad way . . . that's why
we've got to get him to a vet'*

Arthur was wet and cold, and felt very heavy. He was also so exhausted he was almost inert in my arms. I just about managed to pull him on to my lap and then get him into the boat in front of me and onto the bit of mattress as the kayak swayed wildly from side to side.

It was all the more difficult in the pitch dark; our headlamps only lit half the scene. But I was glad of the dark because that way no one could see the tears pouring down my face.

'He's bringing the dog,' came the murmur from the banks behind me. 'Look, look, he's bringing the dog.'

There was a knot in my stomach as I saw how Arthur collapsed in front of me, tongue hanging out, now panting heavily. I could hear one or two people on the bank crying.

Why are they crying? I wondered to myself, as the tears continued to run down my cheeks.

Arthur looked round at me, still panting. Now he was so close, I could clearly see in the light of my headlamp, how bad his wounds were. It was odd to feel his wet fur against my legs and I tried not to think about things like fleas and disease.

But then I told myself that I mustn't think like that. I had made this decision; I could not be afraid of him, or anything to do with him, even if he *did* have fleas and diseases. I had to make him feel welcome, make him feel I trusted him, so that he could trust me.

Arthur seemed to want to turn round and face me, but there wasn't room in the boat.

'Stay still, Arthur,' I said. 'There you go, just sit still.' We had been drifting for a bit now, and the murmurs of the crowd were receding into the distance.

'OK now?' said Simon as he turned to look at his unusual cargo.

'Let's move on,' I said. It was starting to get cold, and it would warm us up to get going after the others. I could see Staffan and Karen up ahead looking back. I couldn't see the expressions on their faces, but imagined Karen looking resigned and Staffan wishing he were back with us in the middle of the action.

'Right, let's get to it,' I shouted to them. 'Coming behind you.'

Simon and I lifted up our paddles again and started to try to get back into some kind of rhythm. But it only took two strokes for me to realise that my technique was never going to work with thirty kilograms of wriggling wet dog between my legs. No part of the paddling motion worked when you had Arthur to accommodate.

I struggled to make the strokes work by half lying on my back, but everything was made twice as hard by the presence of our extra passenger. Yet I found I rather liked the fact that it was all so difficult; it took my mind off worrying about the enormity of what I had done.

Perhaps, I found myself thinking, this is just how it will be from now on. I will try to paddle along as before, but now I must accommodate a new presence. I would have to learn how to paddle differently if Arthur were in my life.

Soon I had started to perfect a different technique, and we were making slightly better progress. The tide was helping us, but we were still struggling to keep up with the others. Arthur had settled down a bit and was now quite still. I wondered how long that would last.

After another hour or so, I saw Karen and Staffan's boat slow down.

'How you doing?' called out Staffan. 'How's Arthur? We should swap, shouldn't we?'

It was true, Simon had done more than his share of struggling with the extra weight. 'We'll swap at that bit of mangrove,' I said as our boat slowed behind them. 'Maybe in the next hour.'

We pushed on, but paddling had got difficult again. Arthur was now obviously restless, and seemed to have recovered a bit from his exertions. He stood up and started looking over the side of the boat, watching the flying fish jump out of the water; he was moving from side to side and sniffing me and Simon and every bit of boat he could reach. Then he started to climb up on the side of the boat, and suddenly there was a splash and he had gone.

'What happened?' said Simon from in front.

'I don't know,' I said. 'He's just gone.' Then I could see him swimming alongside the boat. 'He must have seen something worth chasing in the water.'

I looked down at him again. Arthur was slowing now; he was panting heavily and his head was back down deep in the water. He was starting to whimper a little bit, and I realised that he'd made a mistake. He'd chased after something in the water and hadn't thought through what would happen next. I guess if you're a dog you don't necessarily think of cause and effect in quite the same way as we do.

We slowed the boat again and I leaned over into the water and lifted a cold and wet Arthur back up into the boat again. The sheet of plastic over my legs was coming into its own and protecting me from some of the wet and muck that came into the boat with Arthur.

This time he sat quietly in front of me, but he was now shivering. As it was now the middle of the night the temperature had dropped considerably, and we were all getting colder.

'OK here,' I said as we got near a mangrove island. 'We can stop here and change.' I thought we might all warm up and speed up if two of us changed places.

We pushed the boats up on to the shore. Arthur was looking extra alert at this sudden change of scene, but this time stayed firmly in the boat. Simon went over to Karen's boat, and together they pushed off and started paddling again.

Staffan came over to the front of my boat and we set off behind the others. He immediately started paddling strongly, and we began to make good time compared to the others.

Arthur lay down again once he'd seen what was going on. But he was still shivering uncontrollably. I had two jackets in my pack – a wind jacket and a Gore-tex jacket. I dragged them both out of my backpack and put on the wind jacket. Then I laid the Gore-tex over Arthur, even putting its hood over his head. It didn't fit him exactly, but at least it meant he would have some slightly warmer air round him.

It seemed to do the trick, as he gave a few extra wriggles and then lay still for a bit. Excellent, I thought, he's asleep. Now we can make some progress. We paddled on hard and fast for another two or three hours.

After we'd been going for nearly eight hours, the tide had almost gone out, and navigating the sandbanks it revealed was getting exhausting. It was time for a refuelling stop. There were posts in the river coming up that we could tie ourselves to while we stopped to eat and get a little rest.

It's usually an awkward business anyway, eating and sleeping on a small kayak. But when you're starting to get very tired, and you have a dog on board, it becomes even more so. Staffan and I ate some energy bars and gave a couple of meat sticks to Arthur. We settled down to lie back and try to get some rest. It's difficult enough to sleep in a boat, because you keep losing your balance. But our boat was much more unbalanced than most.

After fifteen minutes or so of trying to sleep, I gave up. Arthur had got all restless again, had wriggled out of his jacket and had somehow manoeuvred himself to the front of the boat. He sat there, all alert and pointing forwards like the captain of the ship or a still from the film *Titanic*.

'Come on then,' I said to the others. 'Let's keep going. Don't stop – let's just do this and get to the finish.'

So we set off again, this time with Arthur at the front of the boat, still looking out to the front, as we got back into our paddling routine. We were making good progress as we approached some rocks on the right-hand side of the river. They led up to a village – we could see there were houses further up the bank from the river – and it looked as if there were people fishing from some of the rocks.

As we got nearer our captain at the front of the boat got restless again. He had his paws on the front of the kayak and was looking over at the rocks. Almost before it happened I knew what he was going to do.

And yes, as we passed the rocks, with a jump and a splash Arthur was in the water again and was soon out and trotting up the rocks towards the village. It was starting to get light now, so I could see him as he got nearer to some of the houses. Then he disappeared behind a wall.

'What's going on?' said Staffan. 'Has he gone, do you think?'

I didn't know what to think. Half of me wanted to think he'd just spotted something he wanted to investigate; the other thought that maybe this was it. Maybe it's over. I looked down at the plastic sheet, the mattress on the bottom of the boat and my filthy jacket. I watched the water that Arthur had brought with him into the boat slosh around as we paddled forwards. And I tried to empty my mind of all thoughts and concentrate on paddling hard.

After about another minute I allowed myself to look back at the bank. No sign of Arthur.

We paddled on silently for another few minutes. I concentrated hard on getting my stroke absolutely in sync with Staffan, and made myself feel pleased by the progress we were making. We were nearly at the end of the rocks that led up to the village by now, so I let myself look up and back towards the bank again.

And there, trotting through the stones that led to the water, was Arthur. As we got nearer he sped up, heading over in our direction.

I found myself grinning like a mad idiot, as we guided the boat gently into the shallow waters. Arthur was now bouncing between the rocks on the shore and moments later was just under the prow of the boat, ready to jump in.

Staffan gave him a helping hand and he pushed past to the middle of the boat and lay down on his mattress as if nothing had happened. I had to put my paddle down to give him a hug. Wet and filthy though he was, he had to know I was glad he was back.

As we headed towards the next checkpoint at the mouth of the river, Arthur went back to his position at the front of the boat. The water was deeper now so the going was a bit easier. Just one more push and we would be landing at the checkpoint.

It was only a short trek from there to the finish line. We pushed on as fast as we could but I knew we had lost so much time over the last three legs. All my plans for making this 'our' bit of the race had rather gone by the board. But as the last checkpoint came into sight, I decided not to think about that. My priority was Arthur, who was now getting restless again as he saw we were getting nearer and nearer to land.

Simon and Karen got there first. They jumped out of their boat and started pulling it up the shore as we landed. Staffan and I got our kit together, grabbed the paddles and, with Arthur following close behind us, we all started to walk the last leg to the finish line in Mompiche.

By comparison with the rest, it was an easy walk, it was daylight, and sleep and real food were within shouting distance, so we kept up a brisk pace until – round a last bend in the road – we saw the big Huairasinchi arch of the finish line.

The five of us walked in a line towards the arch as the officials and crowd gave us claps and cheers. It felt good, and we held hands as we walked across the line and through the arch. It was hard to believe that it was all actually over, that we'd completed the race and we could now stop. Whatever the result, we'd done our best and soon it would be all about recovering and preparing for the next one.

We all gave each other a hug, still slightly shell-shocked.

I was very aware of Arthur padding about in the background as we went through all the checks and congratulations with all the officials. He seemed to be occupying himself inspecting the new smells and sights that you get at a race finish line, but he never allowed himself to be more than a few feet away from us.

We'd dumped our kit with the rest of the boxes of our gear, and gathered round the race organiser to get the low-down on everyone's results.

The winners were Team Seagate, the New Zealanders led by Nathan Fa'avae who we had seen bouncing around the mountains with his children during the pre-race acclimatisation period. Clearly being so used to the altitude had done his team no harm, although they're a good team and are usually in the top three even at sea level. Then came Spain and the Ecuador team, and then four teams from the US, France and Britain who'd clocked in at around the 130-hour mark.

Our score was 146 hours, and twelfth place. OK, but not great. We had made navigation mistakes, we'd had penalties, we hadn't made as much progress as we should have done on a number of the early stages. By the time we'd got to the TA where we met Arthur, we had lost six hours more than we should have done.

Normally I would be going over and over each stage of what had happened. Normally I would already be analysing where we could have made better time, or made fewer mistakes. But this wasn't 'normally', I realised, as I found myself starting to think instead that if we hadn't lost those six hours then I would never have met Arthur.

Perhaps these things happen for a reason.

And then I started worrying about where Arthur was going to sleep that night, what we should feed him and how we were going to get him to a vet.

I found my way to our boxes of gear and got out my cellphone. I didn't feel like I'd landed in the real world yet, but I needed to hear Helena's voice and find out how Philippa was. It was the afternoon in Sweden, so perhaps she'd be sleeping or watching TV. I only had the tiniest bit of battery left, and virtually no signal.

'Hello you.' Helena sounded very faint, but I could just about make out her saying that Philippa was fine and was sleeping; and then she asked about Arthur. Didn't I think that he had all sorts of diseases, everything from fleas and ticks to rabies?

'I guess,' I said. 'Yes. He's in a bad way. That's why we've got to get him to a vet.'

'Okaaaay,' she said. We didn't say much more. I didn't know then that she was already ahead of me. As soon as she had heard that I had taken Arthur into the boat, she had texted Mia, saying, 'So what do you know about bringing dogs into Sweden?!' And as the mother of a beautiful new little daughter she was already thinking far into the future and protecting Philippa.

First, though, it was show time. Helena and the team had done their job well (of course), and had put all the news of us and Arthur up on Facebook as it happened, and had written that our team had 'a fifth member'. Other teams were tweeting about 'the dog,' so there were plenty of people who already knew who the fifth member was as we walked through that arch.

We were allowed time to have a drink and a bit of real food – after so much energy-rich processed food, the thing you pine for at the end of a race is really fresh food like salad and fruit and fresh meat – but then it was time to sit round a table in front of a group of journalists and photographers who were covering the championship.

Arthur followed us to the table, and then immediately settled down for a snooze. He must have thought that with all four of us sitting down it would be safe to take a break from making sure we didn't go anywhere.

The press wanted to know all about Arthur, what had happened, where he'd found us (I was gradually realising that it was Arthur who had found us, not the other way around) and how he'd managed the gruelling trekking and canoeing.

The story was so fresh in my mind, and I loved telling everyone about how he'd tailed us, jumped in the water after us, and stood guard at the front of the boat. Someone asked me if he was coming home with us. I hadn't thought about anything like that, I said; the main thing now was to get him to a vet and get his wounds treated.

Underneath the chat we were sleepless and exhausted, all we could think of was one step at a time. And the next step had to be to get to the hotel and have a wash and sleep.

Nathan Fa'avae and the guys from Seagate told us that the hotel we were booked into didn't have any hot water. Covered as we were with six days' worth of grime, we somehow couldn't face the thought of our first civilised shower being a cold one.

We moved into their hotel instead. It was more expensive than the one we were going to stay in, but Nathan lent us some money to pay the difference. (We may be deadly rivals in a race, but in the real world the deadliest of rivals can be the best of friends.) Once there, we went straight to the room and the showers.

I thought Arthur would want to come in, but there was an outdoor landing on a kind of gallery outside our room, and he seemed happy to sleep on a blanket there. He didn't need an actual bed or a shower, after all, and he was used to being outside.

We went off and all had showers and then crashed. 'Crashing' after a race like this one is an odd and unpredictable affair at the best of times. Apparently your testosterone level drops to roughly the level of that of a twelve-year-old girl. Added to that, your brain is blurry, you have no real conception of night and day and your body is only held together by adrenaline. Once that's stopped kicking in, you gradually become aware of the real stresses and strains you've been under.

Usually, for me, this means a deep but brief sleep – and waking up to find myself aching all over and bathed in gallons of sweat. Quite why the body does this, I don't know; I imagine it's something to do with the way it repairs itself after such extreme pressure.

This time, when I woke from the brief sleep, was no exception. I felt aching, blurry and covered in sweat.

I also had a mass of itches all over my legs.

Arthur. It could only be Arthur. As I scratched my legs till they felt like they were on fire, I realised that Helena was right. Arthur was not only covered in wounds but also home to every flea in the jungle, and we should get him to a vet as soon as possible.

I looked around the room through a mist of tiredness. Simon and Staffan weren't there, but Karen was getting her things together. It was still afternoon, so we headed off into the main town to find something to eat.

As I opened the door, Arthur scrambled to his feet and looked up at me as we got ready to go down the stairs to the sandy road below. It was still hot outside, and as we walked towards the sea there were plenty of people around just sitting outside cafes enjoying the view. Although days and nights had meant nothing to me for the last six days, I realised that that day was a Saturday, and the town was therefore full of normal people enjoying normal weekends. It was an odd thought, and I realised I didn't yet feel like I was back in the real world.

We found a cafe near the beach and sat down. Although Arthur didn't have a lead, he trotted at my heels as if he was on one.

There was another team of racers at the next table eating fish and chips. They looked up as we approached. 'Hey,' one of them called over to us as we sat down. 'What are you doing about the dog? You taking him home?'

I looked down at Arthur as he lay a few inches away from my feet. He was watching people walk by, watching the waiters, but in between always looking up at me just to make double sure I was still there. I looked at the deep wounds on his back, which still looked as bad as they had when I'd first seen him.

'Well, he lives here, I guess,' I said, uncertainly. 'Lives somewhere here anyway. But I've got to get him to the vet. Those wounds are so bad.'

'You know there was some guy who took a dog home once from South America. I think it was quite a famous thing,' the racer said.

'He took him home?' I said. I could feel something inside me skip a beat. 'So you *can* do that?'

'Yeah,' said our friend. 'Think so.' I looked down at Arthur, who now had his head down on his right paw and was giving it a ferocious lick.

At that moment our food arrived – more salad, some cheese, some fresh meat. After I'd given Arthur his share of the meat we got stuck in.

The sleep we'd had seemed to have done nothing to refresh us, and Karen and I didn't say very much as we ate our way through the meal. Almost as soon as I'd finished I stood up to head back to the hotel and more sleep. It was early evening and getting dark. I reckoned I could just about stay awake long enough to have another conversation with Helena, and then I'd be dead to the world.

When I got back to the hotel, my phone was also dead. But just as I was cursing it, Krister came up the stairs to go to his room. Photographers and media people always have machines that work, and he was no exception, so I borrowed his.

I leaned over the balcony outside our rooms and dialled Helena's number. I knew I sounded bleary and very, very tired, but there was something I had to tell her.

'Helena,' I said as soon as she answered. 'We are going to be four. I am going to bring Arthur home.'

There was only the shortest pause before she replied.

'Of course you are,' she said.

Chapter 9

Swedish Aggro

'If Arthur is so committed to us, we will commit to him'

When I woke at dawn the next day I felt exactly as bad as I did when I'd gone to sleep. But there wasn't time to worry about feeling sick or tired, because now I had a new mission and I couldn't afford to waste a second. And this was a mission with a difference: I had less than three days to accomplish it, and I hadn't the faintest idea how to do so.

Our flight back to Stockholm left Quito on Wednesday afternoon. And Helena was going to book Arthur on to that flight. It was now Sunday morning, and it would take the whole of Monday to make the journey from Mompiche to Quito. That gave me effectively forty-eight hours to resolve . . . whatever it was I had to resolve. The more I thought about it, the more I realised what a huge undertaking it was to bring Arthur to Sweden with me – there would be vets, bills, piles of unfamiliar paperwork, complicated logistics, and all in a language I didn't understand. Added to which, I was still terminally exhausted, possibly on the verge of collapse.

As we emerged from the room, blinking into the still-dark dawn, Arthur got to his feet. I supposed that he had slept while we were inside, but it seemed to me that he was always awake, always making sure we were still nearby.

The five of us set off to get something to eat – refuelling with real food would be important in the days to come, I knew that much. I looked at Arthur as he trotted along by my side. No, I thought to myself, you have never had a home, have you? We're so far from where we met, and I can't kid myself you've anywhere to go if you don't come with me. You've staked everything on me, and I can't let you down. Whatever it takes.

Just at that moment Arthur looked up at me. Completely calmly and trustingly. As if he knew what I was thinking, and that somehow he was sure I'd sort it out and we'd always be together.

I bent down and scratched his ear. 'Arthur,' I said under my breath.

We settled down, Arthur sitting at our feet, and ordered some food. Moments later, I saw Krister heading our way.

'OK,' he said, without any of the 'how are you's or 'morning's people usually say. 'It's all kicking off. Everyone's picked up on the TT News story and wants to do an interview. Ecuadorian TV want to do something. Swedish too. Come on, come on, there's no time to lose.'

My brain was just starting to wake up, but all I could think about was who we could get to help with the paperwork and how we could get to a vet in Quito as soon as we got there.

But moments later I found myself back at Krister's hotel – he'd somehow found one with a room with a phone line that worked and which they were making available for interviews. Arthur might have been puzzled by his breakfast being so quickly interrupted, but he followed along behind us as we went to Krister's hotel room.

I charged the phone Krister lent me, and started to try to call back the people who were trying to get hold of us. Helena was reporting an explosion of interest on our media message board, and that our Facebook page was going mad as more and more people picked up on the story.

But the first call I wanted to make was the one to the Swedish Board of Agriculture, the people who decide about animals coming into the country. I was shaking with tension as I looked online for 'Swedish Board of

Agriculture, bringing dogs into the country' and found a phone number.

I was transferred from person to person until finally I found myself talking to someone who actually seemed to understand what I wanted to do and what I needed to know. By this stage I was sounding slightly hysterical even to my own ears, but at last I was talking to someone who didn't seem to think my question was completely mad or a solution completely impossible. She told me I needed to get a vet's check in Ecuador, which involved microchipping and vaccinations, and that all the paperwork should be signed off by the authorities in Quito, and that I should organise quarantine in advance for when we got to Sweden.

It sounded difficult but not impossible. I dialled the number for the quarantine manager that I had been given. There seemed to be only one place that looked after dogs newly arrived in the country: ScandiPet. It was quite near Stockholm and run by a woman called Debbie.

It sounded like a lot would depend on Debbie; my hand shook as I pressed the numbers to call her.

'This is Debbie,' said an American-sounding voice.

'My name is Mikael,' I said. 'I'm calling about a dog called Arthur.' The words, so simple, sounded strange to me. I was holding my breath, literally forgetting to breathe. I felt a bit sick again as I realised that if Debbie couldn't help I had no fall-back plan at all.

'Arthur?' she said. 'The stray dog in Ecuador who's been on the news?'

I breathed out, and smiled. 'Yes,' I said. 'That Arthur.

They said you can help. I'm bringing him to Sweden.' I paused. 'That is, I'm trying to bring him to Sweden. The agri board says he needs to go into quarantine as soon as he gets to Stockholm, and the flight is on Wednesday.'

'Wednesday?' she said. 'Oh my. That's quite soon. But I'm sure people will help you. You'll need him micro-chipped and vaccinated and signed off, as you know. Then he has to be here for four months.'

My heart sank. Four months. We'd only just met and I'd have to say goodbye to him for *four months*?

'How much does it cost?' I said, already dreading the answer.

'About ten thousand kronor a month, depending on vets' bills,' she said. And I felt sick all over again. It was such a huge amount of money, the equivalent of about four thousand pounds. 'But look,' she went on, 'I'd be honoured to help you. Just give what you can.'

'No,' I said. 'That's very kind. But you must have what you're owed. Somehow we'll do it. We will. And thank you. I'd better get going on it all.'

I went back to the hotel and Arthur and the interview room. I had had another twenty missed calls on the other phone while I'd been talking to the agriculture board and to Debbie, and Krister told me there were another three people wanting to interview me. And also more missed calls from *Expressen* and *Aftonbladet* – the two biggest news outlets in Sweden.

But my priority now was how to find a vet and a lot of money.

As captain of Team Peak Performance, I thought, what great PR for them. Peak Performance, a long-established, high-end quality maker of everything you could ever need for the outdoor life, associated with our endurance racing, and now with a wonderful heart-warming story of a man and a dog.

But it was impossible to get through to them, or to anyone who understood what it was I was asking for. Then I thought of the Swedish Armed Forces team, our friendly rivals. With all their boats and planes and manpower, wouldn't it be a great story for them?

They didn't agree, as – perhaps not surprisingly – they took the view that the story should have been about them being the top Swedish team in the race, and not about a stray dog. The other Swedish team, Thule, took rather the same view. So I was starting to despair as I rang Helena to see how she was getting on.

It was evening in Sweden, and she sounded tired, having spent much of the day trying to cope with media phone calls every ten minutes.

'*Aftonbladet* rang eight times while I was trying to change Philippa's nappy,' she said, somehow managing to keep any sign of irritation out of her voice. 'But Mia and Malin are going to help.' I realised that we were going to need them more than ever: everything had started to feel as if it were spiralling out of control. 'The good news,' she continued on the faint and crackly line, 'is that I've booked Arthur into a hotel in Amsterdam.'

I thought one of us had gone a little bit mad.

'What?' I said. 'What hotel?'

'There's a three-hour layover at Amsterdam before your flight to Stockholm,' Helena said. 'He needs to be somewhere nice, not just sitting in his box. So they do these dog hotels for dogs on connecting flights.'

How wonderful, I thought. And how wonderful that Helena's organised that.

Then I thought, but first we've got to find a vet. And the money to pay for it.

I had an idea. I rang *Aftonbladet*, and I rang *Expressen*. I reckoned we needed their help. They said they were sending journalists to cover the story and wanted phone interviews. So Krister and I started to set up some more phone lines that actually worked so that we could get the story out there. If people knew about Arthur, if they could see pictures of him and learn our story, perhaps they could help. Perhaps this huge pressure from the media was a good thing after all.

By the time I collapsed back to bed in the small hours of the following day, I had done back-to-back interviews and made endless phone calls. The news was out there and the world now knew that we needed help with the money to save Arthur.

And I knew, without a shadow of a doubt, that we were *saving* Arthur. Quite apart from the wretched state of his teeth, I had now looked very closely at Arthur's wounds, and they were getting worse. I didn't want to tell Helena – or anyone – but the wounds were infested with ticks and fleas and heaven knows what else. They were getting bigger and nastier. If he didn't get proper help soon, then he would become gradually weaker and weaker as the diseases and parasites overtook him.

I had got our webmaster, Magnus, to set up a 'Help Arthur' appeal page, and by the time I switched off my phone we were already getting masses of responses. And perhaps the best response was Peak Performance saying they would help after all. It looked like we just might be able to raise the money.

With Sweden six hours ahead of Mompiche, the interviews the following day started at 5 a.m. I had had scarcely more sleep in the last couple of days than I'd had during the race, but a new sort of adrenaline seemed to have kicked in, and somehow I found the energy to tell our story to the press countless times in between emailing and calling the authorities about the next stages of the paperwork.

There was also a lot to do after the race. Checking equipment, making sure the gear was ready to ship back, packing and filling in forms, dealing with the organisers. For once in my life I, as captain, wasn't pulling my weight in this regard. I was leaving the others to deal with my kit. And in adventure racing it is an unspoken rule that you deal with your own gear. Staffan was helping me, but Karen had, somewhat understandably, taken a dim view of my preoccupation with Arthur.

'I'm sorry,' I had said to her. 'I know this is not how it should be. But I have to do this. I'm sorry.' It had been all that I could say. And I really was sorry, especially as she was soon going to be flying back to the States and the last thing I had wanted was to have a teammate leave the race angry.

But I also knew that I would do everything in my power to save Arthur and nothing and no one could get in the way of that if I could possibly help it.

Seven interviews with Swedish media later and we were getting ready to leave Mompiche. Staffan, Simon, Karen and most of the athletes set off in the race bus; Arthur and I were going with Krister in his media van. We thought we might see if we could get some of the mud and insect life off Arthur's coat before we spent the day sitting next to him. So Krister found a comb and had a go at pulling some of the dirt out of his fur. It was hard work, and I'm not sure we made much of a difference. I'd just have to have long trousers on and the windows open.

This was undoubtedly Arthur's first experience of being in a car or a van, and it was going to be a long one. It is over 330 kilometres from Mompiche to Quito and a lot of the roads are bumpy and slow going.

But he dealt with it as he seemed to deal with most things, with a deep calm and lack of fuss. We loaded our stuff into the car, and I got into the passenger seat. Arthur settled himself into the footwell by my legs as if he'd been going on long car journeys all his life. Knowing that he couldn't get out of the car must have made him more settled, because there was none of the restlessness that he'd shown on the boat.

We'd been going for about three hours, all of us sitting rather sleepily and silently in the car, when a message reached my phone from the Swedish Board of Agriculture. It informed us that as there would not be a period of twenty-one days between the rabies inoculation and Arthur's entry into Sweden, and as Arthur came from a country outside the EU or any 'permitted' area, it would not be possible for us to 'take the dog into the country'.

I stared in silence at my phone for about a minute, my mouth open in horror. Then I started to swear and curse and shout and then when I ran out of breath I started all over again. Krister eventually managed to get a word in. 'What the . . .?' he said.

'Swedish Agri have said no,' I said. 'They've said no. When before they said it could happen, now they're saying no.'

'OK,' said Krister. 'Keep calm.'

That wasn't the kind of advice I needed. Then I thought, if this is war, then so be it. And I waited until I got a signal on my phone again and dialled the journalists at *Aftonbladet* and *Expressen* I'd been speaking to the previous day.

'Swedish Agri,' I told them both, 'have said no. I can't bring Arthur in. But I'm not giving up. I'm not. I will do whatever it takes. But I am NOT GIVING UP.'

They said they would run the story. They said they would help keep the pressure up.

When we got to Quito we headed straight to the hotel. We needed phones that worked and the chance to get some rest. I had thirty-six hours, maximum, to get Swedish Agri to reverse their decision, find and pay for a vet, get the Ecuadorian and Swedish paperwork, and prepare for us all to get on the plane on the following afternoon.

Meanwhile, Helena and our friends Mia, Malin and Sara in Stockholm had lined up a huge number of interviews for the following morning, with Swedish TV as well as radio and TV in Ecuador. The next day was shaping up to be one of the most important of my life.

We weren't surprised that the hotel in Quito – a lot more upscale than the one in Mompiche – wouldn't allow stray dogs inside. So after we'd had something to eat I settled Arthur into the van as best I could. Knowing how important smells are to dogs, I took off my shirt and put it in the footwell so that Arthur would be able to smell me during the night. We would have to keep him shut in, so I wanted him to feel as safe as I could make him. I felt bad about shutting up a dog who was used to roaming about an entire country, but I was only reckoning on two or three hours' sleep, so it wouldn't be for very long.

Coming down into the hotel lobby the following morning was like arriving at an airport when all the flights had been cancelled. There seemed to be dozens of people milling around, all wanting to be at the head of the queue.

I slipped out of a side door and went out to the van to fetch Arthur. As usual, he was wide awake and waiting for me, making little whimpering noises from behind the passenger door. He jumped out, and jumped all over me. I had a piece of rope that the hotel had given me to double as a lead, but Arthur was sticking to my side like glue anyway, so I hardly needed to use it.

We made our way back to the forecourt in front of the hotel where all the journalists were waiting. As they saw us approaching, they started shouting questions to us in Spanish. Thinking how I couldn't understand a word of what was, after all, Arthur's language, I suddenly had a surreal thought: how would Arthur cope with learning Swedish, one of the most difficult languages in the world?

Then the cameras started clicking and flashing, louder and louder as we got nearer. And I got back to focusing on what I needed to say about our dilemma; how we needed help to get Arthur out of Ecuador and into Sweden. Two hours later and we were just finishing talking to a Spanish-speaking radio station when a young guy in jeans and a white shirt tugged at my sleeve.

'Hi,' he said confidently, with a grin. 'I'm Ismael Carrión. I think I can help.'

'Can you?' I said. No one had ever sounded like they knew all the answers like this guy did. 'Can you really?' I felt a small surge of hope. He seemed so at home in the media melée, but also so sure of himself.

He bent over to say hello to Arthur, and scratch behind his ears.

'He's a great fellow, isn't he?' said Ismael. 'He seems so calm. In all this noise and mess too. But he's in a bad way.'

I watched him investigate Arthur's wounds, and his teeth and ears, and was reminded all over again about how urgent it was to get him to a vet.

'It's bad for dogs in this country,' Ismael said. 'I'm not surprised at the state of him. So many street dogs here in Ecuador. And nobody stops them being mistreated. So they just end up sick and wounded like this.'

He looked up at me. 'If you're serious about taking him to Sweden, there's a lot to do. Like, first we get him to the vet. Follow me.'

As we followed him out of the hotel grounds, I looked round at Staffan, Simon, Krister and Karen and found myself smiling broadly. Somehow Ismael's confidence was rubbing off on me. Ismael explained that he worked for an animal centre called Lord Guau where they looked after dogs, doing everything for them from grooming and day care to travelling and vet care, and that he was going to lead us to the twenty-four-hour vet.

We got back in the van and navigated our way round the streets of Quito until we came to a big building that had the reassuring words 'Hospital Veterinario' over the door. Staffan led the way with Arthur on his piece of rope. As I followed with Ismael, I could see that there were cameras waiting for us even here.

We were greeted by two nurses and a vet. I guess everyone in Quito knew who Arthur was by now, because they crowded round him as if he were some kind of film star.

But they were also very caring and professional. They took his paws, checking for cuts, they tied a strap round him and took some blood, they parted all the matted fur on his back and looked at the wounds.

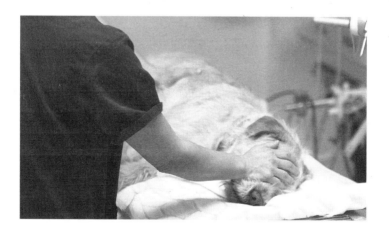

Through all this Arthur remained totally calm. The last three or four hours had been extraordinary for him – they'd been extraordinary for me too – but he seemed completely accepting of everything that happened to him and all the attention and noise that seemed to accompany him everywhere he went.

Ismael was talking to the doctors all the time Arthur was being examined. As the nurses started to clean Arthur's wounds he turned to me and said, 'They're going to sedate him. They've got to clean those wounds as much as they can. They're infected and infested. And also clean his mouth – those teeth are in a very bad way. They say he needs a proper operation but, for now, they can at least give him disinfectant.'

I thought 'disinfectant' sounded a bit brutal, but hoped it was just lost in the translation, and all they were going to do was clean up the wounds with antiseptic.

'And then they will put a microchip in him, and give him a rabies shot,' Ismael went on. 'We need all these certificates for the paperwork at the airport.'

'But surely,' I said as they started to get Arthur ready for his mini-surgery, 'no one in Ecuador needs paper-work. After all, we're taking him out of the country, not trying to bring him in.'

'You wouldn't believe,' said Ismael. 'It's crucial we get the OK from the Ecuadorian Agriculture Board.'

My heart sank again. So far we'd been told by the Swedish agri board that we couldn't bring him into Sweden; what if the Ecuadorian one told us we couldn't take him out?

I put that out of my mind and concentrated on the sight of Arthur going into a small room on an operating table.

He looked so helpless and vulnerable, I had to keep reminding myself that he was safe now, and this was all for his own good.

I went to the waiting room and sat down with the others, unable to concentrate on anything anyone was saying. All I wanted was for Arthur to be all right.

Chapter 10

Mongrel Dog

Name: Arthur
Sex: Male
Age: 8

Arthur was only in surgery for half an hour or so, but to me – sitting in the cramped waiting room with the rest of the team and assorted cameramen and journalists – it felt like hours.

When he came out, part of his back was painted grey where the wounds were, and I could see his gums were bright red where I presumed they'd been treated. He also had a plastic collar round his neck to stop him trying to lick his dressings. But other than that he looked like the same Arthur, just with slightly cleaner fur.

'OK boy?' I said as I scratched the special place behind his ear that he seemed to like having scratched.

He looked back up at me, tongue hanging out, panting, but seemingly quite calm. It was extraordinary how nothing seemed to upset or worry him – maybe it was because he knew now that I'd be there to look after him. Maybe all these things happening to him were as nothing compared to the terrible things that had happened to him earlier in his life. I tried not to think about that, and just gave him another bit of a cuddle.

Ismael and the doctor and a nurse with a clipboard and a pen then went into the corner with several sheets of paper. I could see they were filling in forms and signing things and handing more bits of paper over to Ismael, talking fast in Spanish as they did so. I couldn't understand a word they were saying, but somehow I felt they were all acting together and in our interests. As if they were filling in the forms to get whatever the 'right' result was. Whatever it takes, I found myself thinking again. And also, how grateful I was for the help.

'Right. Now we're going to Lord Guau,' said Ismael, leading the way out of the vet hospital.

When we got to Lord Guau, we were welcomed by the owner and led into what looked like an enormous garden.

It was full of dogs and had kennels and stalls with dog equipment for sale round the edges.

Arthur was looking slightly uncomfortable in his plastic collar, but it didn't stop him submitting to being interviewed and photographed at the entrance and in the garden. Everything we did, it seemed, was being recorded and filmed.

Ismael led us to the place where we could buy Arthur a lead. I chose a black one with lots of ways to adjust the length, and which went round Arthur's shoulders as well as his neck. I thought that since this was probably Arthur's first ever proper lead it needed to be comfortable as well as smart. Then we got him a plastic bone he could practise chewing on – I thought that might help his teeth – and then we chose his travelling kennel.

This was going to be his home for the two days it would take to get him to Stockholm and quarantine. We chose a very smart blue one, with as big an opening to it as we could find; I wanted Arthur to be able to see out as much as possible. As I looked at it, still reeling from the news that we might be facing problems from Ecuador as well as Sweden, I hoped against hope that he would get to use it.

We took our new purchases – which I later realised weren't purchases at all but kind gifts from the centre – to a cafe nearby. It was Ismael's recommendation and it served wonderful fresh sushi. It was the first fresh food I'd had since those two meals at Mompiche, and very good it tasted too. I didn't seem to have had any more time for eating – or sleeping – than I had had when I was in the middle of the race. Perhaps it was no wonder that I was still feeling stiff with exhaustion.

The next stop was Quito Airport and the Ecuadorian Agricultural Board officials. Staffan and Simon were going to return the van to the hire centre, so Arthur, Krister and I went with Ismael to the airport.

I spent most of the journey checking my phone. *Aftonbladet* and *Expressen* had been as good as their word and the stories about my struggle to bring Arthur to Sweden, and the agriculture board preventing us, was given lots of column inches. Lots of column inches.

As we rolled up to the perimeter of the airport another message came through. It was from Helena and Mia in Stockholm. They had heard from my original contact at the Swedish Board of Agriculture. The message was simply 'OK, OK, stop giving us a hard time. We will sort this.'

I gazed at my phone and felt a silly grin come over my face. 'Hey,' I said to Ismael. 'I think it might be OK. Swedish Agri have said they are going to give us permission.' I looked at Arthur, sitting by my feet. 'I think it's going to be all right,' I said again to him.

'That's great,' said Ismael. There was no time to worry about whether or not the Swedish Agri Board really would 'sort this', because moments later we were at the airport and following Ismael towards the section for customs and imports and the agricultural office. It was a small room with three people in it and various piles of paperwork all over the table.

Ismael handed in all the documentation for Arthur. Krister and I stood behind him, listening to the conversation but of course unable to understand a word. Everyone was talking at breakneck speed, but nobody seemed to be agreeing on anything. It was all going on a lot longer than it should have done, given that we had all the paperwork signed by the vet.

I looked down at Arthur, standing patiently by my side not making the slightest bit of fuss about all the strange things that were happening to him, and thought again how he seemed to trust that somehow it would be all right so long as he was with me.

After another minute of gesticulation and arm-waving, Ismael broke off to turn round and say to me, 'Not good. They say they can't authorise.'

I felt my heart sink – that same sick, empty feeling that I'd had when I had the message from the Swedish Board of Agriculture saying no.

Ismael was talking again to the people behind the desk. He wasn't shouting, but you could tell that he was getting angry; but all three of the officials looked utterly unforgiving and stern. They weren't saying very much but even I could understand the word 'no' in Spanish.

Suddenly Ismael turned round to us and said, 'OK, they're not moving. We can't do anything here. We go.' And he led the way out of the office and out of the airport.

We made our way in silence to the car. It was getting dark by now, which seemed somehow appropriate as we walked through the jumbled streets back to the centre of Quito. It would soon be time for the official closing ceremony of the Championship – which I had to go to, not least because I needed to see Nathan Fa'avae to pay him back the money we owed him from the hotel in Mompiche – and it was starting in less than an hour.

'But what more can we do? He's got the chip and the shots, what more can we do?' I said, feeling despair as we drove back from the airport.

'We figure something out,' said Ismael. 'But now we have to take him to the police.' I had a strange vision of Arthur being arrested. Being locked up in jail.

'What do you mean, police?' I said.

'They say he must be in care of the State,' said Ismael. I wasn't sure if he was being serious or not, but then, as we drove up to a big gateway with a sign saying 'Policia', I realised that he was.

Ismael talked to the two officers at the entrance to the building. I wished I understood some Spanish, any Spanish. But they seemed friendly and helpful, so I began to hope that Arthur wouldn't be arrested after all.

We could hear a lot of barking coming from the other side of the building. After a minute or two Arthur obviously couldn't resist and let out a big woof, just to show he was there too.

The officers then led us into a courtyard at the back of the building, which was surrounded on all sides by dog kennels. It was even noisier here, but there were empty kennels along one side of the courtyard and they seemed to be signalling to us that this was where Arthur was going to spend the night.

There was a water bowl in the corner and another, empty, bowl. One of the officers reached up to some packs of dog food on a high shelf and poured some meat and biscuits into the empty bowl. He took off Arthur's plastic collar and watched Arthur as he headed purposefully to the bowls.

'We must go,' said Ismael. 'There is work to do.'

I looked back at Arthur, already halfway through the food in his bowl, and then I looked at the policemen. They were obviously used to looking after dogs. And anyway we had no choice but to leave him in their care.

We headed back to the hotel. There were emails coming in every minute, and our Facebook pages were bursting with activity and messages. And for Helena and Mia, Malin and Sara it was even busier.

The story of Arthur had now spread way beyond Sweden and Ecuador, and there were American and English journalists and broadcasters who wanted to talk to me and follow the story.

The appeal for money on the makeshift website had now exceeded all our hopes. With Peak Performance having now offered to help, it looked like the appeal would be well into credit.

Ismael had been telling us a lot about how stray dogs in Ecuador were treated. It wasn't only that so many were kicked, beaten or starved, it was also that many people in Ecuador didn't have any sense of responsibility for pets in general and dogs in particular. They'd get a dog, decide they wanted it to have puppies, couldn't deal with the puppies, and so the puppies would just be left to roam the streets. And there they were mistreated and starving – and so the cycle continued. It can happen all over the world, of course, but in Ecuador it wasn't officially a crime to mistreat animals, and there wasn't an obligation to look after them, register or sterilise them. So the whole dreadful situation was perpetuated.

'It's wonderful what you try to do for Arthur,' Ismael said as we drove back to the centre of town. 'Always good when dogs are rescued, also when charities feed and look after them. But it is no cure for the problem. It's like using an aspirin to cure cancer. It makes the pain go away but you're not going to cure it.'

I decided that whatever happened, I would do what I could to help. If it was money to support Ismael and others like him who were trying to get the law changed, or to help individual stray dogs, then there must be a way I could help.

But first we had a million calls to make and emails to write. We were still on tenterhooks about the Swedish Board of Agriculture's decision – all we had was a friendly message from my contact there, nothing in writing – and now we had to persuade the Ecuadorian equivalent to let Arthur on to the plane.

Ismael headed off to make some calls, but I had to break off and get ready for the closing ceremony.

I only just made it in time. The ceremony was just about to start as I got to the entrance to the Museum of Water, where Nathan and his team were going to be crowned champions of champions. The museum is a spectacular building overlooking the city of Quito. Seemingly made of nothing but glass, steel and water, it backs on to some spectacular mountains and has tremendous views out towards El Panecillo – the famous hill with the giant stone Madonna monument at its top.

The atmosphere was buzzing, with newly clean but still hyped athletes celebrating the end of what had been a pretty amazing race. Mostly everyone agreed that the altitude had been a problem, but that it was a well-planned race and had taken in some pretty impressive sights.

But after I'd slapped Team Seagate on the back and paid Nathan the money we owed, I couldn't wait to get back to my hotel and the huge task ahead of me that was dominating every second of my thoughts.

A couple of hours later and, through Helena and the team in Sweden, I had talked to five more journalists, and was beginning to feel that there couldn't be a person in the world who didn't know about our struggle. All the time, every second of the evening, people were asking for pictures, comments, stories, answers to questions, questions, questions . . .

Then Mia came through with a message of some hope. The Minister for Social Development in Ecuador had heard of the story. Perhaps, we thought, there was a chance that someone that powerful could help.

I kept coming back to the fact that we weren't trying to introduce an animal to Ecuador, we were taking one away. How could that be a problem?

Then I thought of Arthur, in his police kennel. I thought of him with his bowl of food now empty, and none of us around him.

Ridiculous, I told myself. As Ismael had said, clearly Arthur was a loner, and had survived on his own – when he found us he was on his own, and he never interacted with any other dogs – and he would never have travelled in a pack. So why should I be worried about him being on his own?

Because now we were his pack. With me as its captain. And now we were his only hope.

I tried to push all thoughts of Arthur in his police kennel out of my mind. I must focus, focus. The only hope was that somebody in a position of authority could change the position with the Ecuadorian Agricultural Board, someone who could wave a magic wand and where they had said no, get them to say yes. And the only way we could effect that would be by getting massive coverage for our story. In the hope that someone somewhere could help us.

I was beginning to despair, sitting in my hotel room with my head in my hands, when Helena phoned and said she had had a message from someone connected to the Minister for Social Development in Ecuador asking what needed to happen to get Arthur out of the country. Helena had told them that we needed the Ecuadorian Agriculture Board at the airport to allow Arthur to get on the plane to Stockholm. We needed the people who had said no to say yes.

The person Helena was talking to had said that it was probably possible to arrange that, given that Arthur had had all the jabs and was microchipped, and the best thing we could do was to take him with us to the airport tomorrow, go straight to the people we'd seen that day and ask them to reverse their decision. This person then went on to say that at their end she would ensure that today's no would be tomorrow's yes.

I breathed out. So it was just possible that the someone powerful who I'd prayed for might come to the rescue. I called Ismael. What did he think? Was it possible that this was the miracle we'd hoped for?

Ismael reckoned that it might well be, and we would just have to carry on and hope.

Carrying on and hoping was very hard. I was absolutely stiff with exhaustion, but there were still calls to return and photos to send and questions to respond to. But I was by now so completely exhausted that if there were to be any hope at all of making this happen the following morning, I needed to get at least an hour or two's rest. It was midnight. I set my alarm for 5 a.m.

But I didn't need to wait for my alarm to sound, I was woken by the buzzing of my phone. It was Helena.

'Hey,' she said. 'Go and look at your computer. I've sent you something that's just come through for you.'

Blearily I tried to ask whether it was good news or bad news, but she wasn't telling me, and hung up. I switched on the laptop. Her email simply consisted of a copy of a formal letter from the Swedish Board of Agriculture. It said:

Decision
The Agricultural Board approves your application and allows import from Ecuador to Manlötens quarantine of the following animal:

Dog: mongrel; Name: Arthur; Sex: male; Age: 8

There followed a long list of conditions and items of paperwork that were part of their permission. But I couldn't read a word of them right at that moment. In fact I couldn't see anything at all. The tears were streaming down my face as I put my head in my arms and cried like a baby.

By the time the sun came up that morning of D-Day – the day of departure for Sweden one way or the other – I was packed, anxious and ready to go. As I walked downstairs to the lobby, I was clutching a printout of the Swedish permit like it was some sort of talisman.

There were crowds of reporters all around the entrance and exits of the hotel, but we needed to go to pick up Arthur straight away, so Staffan, Simon and I ducked round and out of the back entrance to join Ismael. There was no time for more interviews, and anyway I just wanted to get to the police kennels.

It seemed to take ages to get to the police station. As I looked out of the car window at a traffic jam up ahead, I thought how incredible it was that this time last week I hadn't even met Arthur, and yet here I was beside myself with anxiety about him. Rigid with fear that somebody, somehow, would stop us spending the rest of our lives together.

He couldn't have gone through all that pain and exhaustion to find me only for it all to come to nothing. He couldn't.

The more I thought about it the more I felt that we were meant to be together. Whether I believed in destiny or not – and sometimes I do and sometimes I don't – I *knew* we were meant to be together.

I looked again at the permit in my hand. It said yes, the permit said yes. If only the vets at the airport would say the same.

When we arrived at the police station, I thought that in the light of day the kennels looked smaller and less intimidating. Maybe Arthur hadn't had such a bad night after all. Then I heard a familiar woof. As we opened the door to the kennel there was Arthur, tail almost a blur as he jumped up at me.

The police had put more of the grey antiseptic on his back, so the grey was now quite dark against his golden fur. He did look pretty battered still, so I put his new lead around him carefully, keeping away from his wounds.

We had loaded up the van that Ismael had organised for the journey to the airport with all our gear – mountains of race kit, and also Arthur kit; his big blue travelling kennel took up most of the space. There was only just room for one dog, if he sat quietly in the front by my feet.

But this time he didn't sit quietly. Unlike on the journey from Mompiche, Arthur was now all fidget and restlessness. He seemed to be very excited, almost as if he knew something big and important was going to happen that day.

I told the others about the miracle email I'd had in the middle of the night. 'I want to send chocolates, flowers, something to the woman at Swedish Agri,' I said as we set off through the streets of Quito. 'But there's no time, it's all so crazy. Crazy.'

'It's the Ecuadorian minister you need to send chocolates to now,' said Staffan. 'Supposing they still say no at the airport?'

'They *can't* say no,' I said, gripping Arthur's lead so tightly that the whites of my knuckles showed. I felt a painful ache in my stomach; the stress was really getting to me. 'How can they stop us leaving, how can they? I don't understand.'

'OK, OK,' said Ismael. 'It should be all right. We've got all the right papers, and now we've got proof from Sweden. The call should work.'

When we arrived at the airport I couldn't believe the number of people gathered round the entrance – dozens and dozens of them. Most of them had microphones or cameras, but lots of them didn't. It was like the reception a pop band would get, a mixture of fans and press.

We got out of the van and were immediately surrounded. At the front was a group of young Ecuadorian girls who just dropped to their knees and put their faces up to Arthur. One of them was practically kissing him. And then other people started putting their hands towards him, patting him, stroking him or just touching him. It was like he was some kind of holy person, I thought, like a kind of canine Mother Teresa. It was extraordinary.

But as always, Arthur took it all in his stride. When some-one stroked him he wagged his tail, and when another young woman put her face next to his he gave it a little gentle lick.

The crowd was ten deep as we made our way slowly, slowly to the office where the people who would decide our fate were based. It was a small office, but I could see it was already completely surrounded by press and Arthur fans.

We only had about half an hour at the most before we had to check in and go through to Departures. Surely, I thought to myself, with all these witnesses, they can't stop Arthur coming with me.

With my half of the paperwork in my hand, I followed Ismael into the tiny office. There was only just room for the four of us, Arthur, and two or three cameramen as we approached the desk. The three officials were the same ones as the day before, and if anything they looked even more unfriendly and cross than they had then.

Ismael spoke to them firmly and quickly in Spanish. The expressions on their faces took on an even grimmer hue. They started to answer him, just as quickly and firmly. They went on like this for five long minutes. As I watched them, knotted up with tension, I felt the pain in my stomach get worse.

Then one of them made a phone call. And then, still looking grim, they took all the papers we gave them and put them down on their desk. I felt that if it were at all possible they would have taken the greatest pleasure in throwing them away and sending us out of their office. But whoever the blessed person was from the ministry, and at the end of the phone, and bless Ismael too, they started to sign and stamp the papers.

Ismael turned to me as the last paper was stamped, with a great big grin on his face.

'We've done it,' he said. 'You can go and check in.'

I could hardly believe it. I knew that Ismael's grin was as nothing compared to mine.

'Hey.' I bent down to Arthur. 'Hey, boy, we've done it! Did you hear that? You're coming with me. You and me, we're going to Sweden!'

I put my face right up against his and kissed his funny heart-shaped nose. He licked me right back. Suddenly I didn't feel tired and stiff any more, I just felt happy.

I rang Helena with the good news. She had been on tenterhooks too, and her tension had somehow transferred itself to Philippa who had been uncharacteristically restless and sleepless all day. Helena had had to spend most of the afternoon taking her for walks, but always, always hanging on the phone.

I knew now that ever since she had heard that I had pulled Arthur into the boat, she had known that I would want to bring him home. She knew that before I did.

It was late by now in Örnsköldsvik, but of course she was wide awake and so happy for us all. 'So good he's got his hotel at Amsterdam, isn't it?' she said. 'Malin and Mia and I will work on what happens in Stockholm. The press here are going to go mad when you arrive.'

I knew that was true, but couldn't think about it just then. I was still exploding with relief that we'd made it, and Arthur was going to be on the plane. 'Kisses to you and Philippa,' I said, exhilarated and exhausted at the same time. 'See you in Stockholm.'

The airline and its staff were milling around and guiding us all to a special check-in area. Staffan and Simon went ahead with the giant boxes of our kit, and I walked behind with Arthur. Our progress was incredibly slow; it took more than half an hour to walk 100 metres, because there were just so many people who wanted to say hello and goodbye to Arthur. Everyone wanted a photograph, a pat, a lucky stroke of his head.

As we finally went through the departure gates, I gave Ismael a hug. 'Thank you for everything,' I said.

'No problem,' he answered, as if he saved a life every day.

Then it was time to lead Arthur gently into his box. He was quite quiet now, as if he knew he had a long and strange ordeal ahead of him. He went in backwards so that he was looking at me till the last possible moment. 'You'll be fine, you'll be fine,' I said to him as we did up the front of the box.

I stood up as the officials came forward to take his kennel through to the luggage area, and as they carried it out to the aeroplane, I shouted, 'I'll see you in Sweden, Arthur!'

Chapter 11

New Home, Old Wounds

'He was very calm . . . I didn't think
he was going to be so calm'

The three of us went through to passport control, rather subdued after so much tension and excitement. We were all exhausted, especially me after so much stress and so little sleep, but Simon too. After all, he had had a tough time of it being so dehydrated on the race, and he'd done extraordinarily well to make it to the finish line.

The journey out to Ecuador seemed like it had happened in another world. Back then I had been sitting with my team plotting and strategising every last leg of the race, planning how we were going to make the last three stages 'ours' and overtake the competition. And now here we were just a few days later, having lost crucial hours in the race, but having gained a new member of the family.

I smiled at the thought. Perhaps I looked a little goofy to the officer checking my passport, but I didn't really care and by then could only think of sleep, wonderful sleep.

The flight to Amsterdam took fourteen hours. And I wasn't conscious for any of them. We landed at about 1p.m. Dutch time, and had four hours to kill before the connection to Stockholm. All three of us were slightly dazed as we headed out into AMS Airport. We had our very own sort of jetlag; the time wasn't the issue, it was more that we were still in recovery mode from the last ten days.

I was so glad that Helena had fixed it for Arthur to be looked after for these few hours. Although I was gradually coming to the conclusion that he could take pretty well anything in his stride, he had nevertheless been in an aeroplane hold in a small box for over a day. He would need fresh air, food and a walk.

Deciding not to worry about him, I led the others to a likely looking airside restaurant that we could make our base camp to talk about what had gone before and what was to come.

Since the news of Arthur's being allowed to come to Sweden had been announced on the Internet and the news channels, everything had exploded in the media. There was going to be a lot of press at Stockholm and a lot of interviews.

Sadly, and ironically given that we had won our struggle to be together, I would then have to say goodbye to Arthur. Although not for that long, I kept telling myself; at least I would see him from time to time during the four months of his quarantine. And he and Helena and Philippa would get to know each other a little bit before he finally came home for good.

I was just starting to worry about the cost of it all – while in quarantine he was going to be a flight and a car hire away – when Staffan burst in on my thoughts.

'So,' he said. 'What happens when we land then?'

'Chaos, my friend,' I said. 'Media circus. Helena is trying to get a permit to film in the airport. Apparently that's an issue. And Malin and Mia are fielding a call every second about us.' This was turning out to be Sweden's biggest news story in ages. Apparently they were going to broadcast our arrival at Stockholm Airport live, the kind of thing they would normally only do for a state visit, a movie star or the return of a winning national hockey team.

'We need to have our hair brushed and our teeth clean, because we will be all over the media,' I said to the others. The more I thought about it, the more unbelievable it all was. But so long as we could get Arthur safely into the country and into Debbie's hands it would all work out fine. I knew from the first time I'd heard Debbie speak that Arthur would be safe with her; it was a gut feeling, and I always trusted my gut.

After several more coffees, we headed back to the departure gates. It was only a two-hour flight to Stockholm, so it wouldn't be long before I would see Helena and Philippa, and actually be in Sweden with Arthur.

The calls to Malin and Mia went on right up until take-off. Was I ready? they asked. Did I know where to go? Did I realise quite what a big deal this was going to be? Was I prepared for flashing lights and TV interviews?

Not really, I felt like saying. But whatever it takes.

As soon as we landed we were herded towards the luggage belts and our equipment boxes. I was taken to one side and told to wait by a separate entrance that joined the landing strip to the Arrivals hall. It was a kind of tunnel leading into the baggage hall.

And then there it was. Arthur's kennel, on the back of a luggage wagon, was heading towards us. As it got nearer I felt a little wave of excitement. A bit like you might get on a first date.

'Don't forget,' said an airport official by my side. 'You

can't let him out. He has to go to quarantine without leaving his kennel. That's the law.'

They turned the kennel round so the front was facing me. And there was Arthur. Tongue hanging out. Panting a bit. But looking just the same as ever after twenty-three long hours.

When he saw me he started to whimper a little and wriggle. 'Hey, Arthur,' I said, putting my fingers through the wire front of the kennel so he could lick them, 'Welcome to Sweden. You're safe now, Arthur. You're with us.'

There wasn't time to say any more. Our luggage was coming off the special 'outsize' belts and we needed to get everything on trolleys so we could exit into Arrivals in one go.

'Ready?' said Mia on the end of the phone. 'Better be prepared for a bit of a fuss!'

'OK,' I said. 'No worries,' I added, not really meaning it.

And so we set off. I led the way, with Arthur's kennel on top of a box of gear, all on one huge trolley.

The automatic exit doors drew back and revealed a scene of absolute mayhem. Dozens of people and cameras flashing from every direction. Lots of shouting, and banks of people everywhere you looked.

And there at the front of everyone, coming towards me: Helena with Philippa in her arms. It was so wonderful to see them, but I only had time for a quick kiss before we were engulfed by people, cameras and microphones.

We were moved to the side of the Arrivals area, where we were instantly surrounded by press ten deep. Question after question was shouted at me, and I answered them as best I could. But all the time I was terribly aware that Arthur was in his kennel wriggling and whimpering a little bit and wondering why he wasn't allowed out.

I was just telling TT News about the scenes at Quito Airport when I saw out of the corner of my eye someone go up to Arthur's kennel and start fiddling with the catch to the door. That someone was Staffan. Before I knew it he'd opened the door and out came Arthur.

He seemed pleased to be out and started to come towards me, as if to say, *What was all that about?* I put a lead round him and looked reproachfully at Staffan. After all, we had gone through hell and high water to get to this stage. What if the authorities said we'd broken the conditions of quarantine?

But Staffan just shrugged. 'What could I do?' he said. 'Arthur wanted to come out. He's been in there so long, and people wanted to see him.'

Now that he was outside Arthur seemed totally calm again. He just surveyed the chaos – the flashing lights, the shouting, the people pushing each other to get better photos – and gave himself a little shake.

I was aware that Aftonbladet TV were filming every-thing, so I was worried that there was proof for all to see of Arthur having been illegally allowed out.

Helena and Philippa were at my side now, and I

managed to give each of them a hug. I think Philippa was a little bit tense, but she looked hard at Arthur as he padded about being made a fuss of by all those people. 'Ulv,' she said hesitantly. I thought this was good. Philippa was only small and didn't have many words yet, but 'wolf' was a good start. I had a feeling that Arthur was going to be 'Ulv' to her from now on.

Helena and I smiled at each other as Philippa hesitantly put her hand out towards him. Helena had been showing Philippa pictures of Arthur and tried to explain that he would soon be coming home with us. It was beginning to look like it had worked.

The TV crews were now crowding around, anxious to get their interview slots recorded, and it was all getting very hectic. There was also a certain famous boxer and mixed martial arts fighter who'd arrived on the same flight as we had, who was contributing to the chaos by refusing to believe that the fuss wasn't all about him.

It did amuse us that an Ecuadorian stray dog had hogged the limelight from Alexander Gustafsson, light heavyweight champion, aka 'the Mauler'.

After more than an hour of telling our story to radio and TV reporters and posing with each other and Arthur, I was beginning to feel exhausted all over again. And I was now desperate to meet Debbie and talk to her properly. I'd been told she was standing in the background of the crowd during that last interview, waiting patiently to be introduced to Arthur and do her job, but the press

It was so hard being away from Arthur, especially when I knew he was alone in quarantine and distressed from his surgeries.

Helena and Philippa came too, and it was wonderful to see Philippa get more and more used to Arthur. Arthur loved Helena from the start.

We stayed with Arthur until dark. It was heart-breaking to leave him.

You can't explain to a dog that you'll come back.
But I hope that Arthur trusted I would.

Arthur's teeth were still in a bad state and causing him a lot of pain.

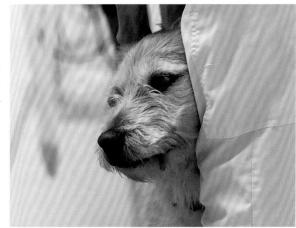

He had operations in Ecuador and then a bigger one in Sweden to fix his teeth. It must have been scary for him – I know it was for me.

But you can't keep a good dog down!

The day I could tell him we were finally bringing him home
was one of the happiest days of my life.

Finally, we were home, and Arthur settled into family life quite quickly.

It wasn't long before Philippa and Arthur became the best of friends.

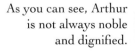

As you can see, Arthur is not always noble and dignified.

Here's Arthur with the same type of meatballs I gave him when we first met. He turned his nose up at them this time!

But some things stay the same – Arthur and I still like to go for runs together.

Arthur is an adventurer
t heart.

But I think perhaps
an adventurous
spirit runs in the
family.

Arthur's first Christmas in Sweden, and Thor's first Christmas.

Arthur is such a part of our family now, we can't imagine life without him.

were never-ending in their requests for stories, comments, more stories and more pictures.

I knew it was all in a good cause. After all, the more publicity Arthur's plight was given, the better for the cause of all stray dogs in Ecuador – and in South America and the world generally. But I was only too aware that things can go very wrong if you rely too much on the goodwill of the media.

Already, Mia said, we had had people making negative comments because we had been described in the press as 'Sweden's adventure racing team', which, understandably, annoyed the other Swedish adventure racing teams. But you couldn't explain to each and every fan that some parts of the press had a policy of not mentioning brands like Peak Performance, so they just called us 'the Swedish team'.

Over the years Helena and I had had a great deal of publicity in the Swedish press, which was good for our team and our sponsors but sometimes not so nice for Helena when people wanted to shoot us down for the sake of it. I think I've got a thicker skin than she has, but it's never nice to be held up to ridicule or criticism for something you haven't done or hadn't intended. We've never read a story in the press about something we really, really know about that's got everything right. I'm sure most people find that.

But, of course, right now we never stopped being grateful for the attention Arthur had got in the media. At certain moments in the last crazy few days, they had made all the difference, in a good way.

Finally, we were through. The press were directed out of the airport area, and we were free to talk to Debbie and hand Arthur over to her care. Debbie seemed exactly as calm and professional as she'd sounded on the phone.

'I think those wounds are still really bad,' I said to her as we manoeuvred Arthur back into his kennel. 'And his teeth – well, tell me what you think when you have a chance, but I think he actually finds eating uncomfortable. He's missing most of his front teeth. It looks . . . it doesn't look good.'

'Don't worry,' said Debbie firmly and confidently, taking all the hard-earned documents and permits from my hand. 'We'll look after him and check everything out.'

'OK,' I said.

Although I had prepared myself emotionally for this moment, it was still hard, very hard, to have to say goodbye to Arthur when we'd only just arrived. But I kept telling myself it was all for his own good. 'And visiting? How do we do that? When can we see him?'

'Well,' said Debbie, 'Not too often. It unsettles a dog if they keep seeing you and you keep going away. But we'll sort out a schedule. Let's just see how he settles down.'

There were only a few minutes to go before we had to check in for our flight home to Örnsköldsvik. Which was perhaps just as well because, despite my good intentions, I was starting to feel very sad about waving goodbye to Arthur.

Then I turned back to Helena, standing patiently with Philippa sitting in her arms, and I felt better. We could go home now, be together, and start to think about getting ready to make a new home for Arthur.

The first week home after a full-length championship race is always a period of strange adjustment. You become painfully aware of any injuries, you are still bleary from lack of proper sleep and you feel you want to gorge on proper, fresh, real food.

But this particular re-entry to 'normal' life was odder than ever. I was deeply exhausted, not just from the race, but from the sleeplessness and worry about whether we would be able to bring Arthur home.

I realised that I was very lucky to have so much stamina and willpower, or I might have had some kind of breakdown during those frantic hours in Mompiche and Quito.

To begin with it was very hard to calm down. In my heart of hearts I knew that Arthur was still in a very bad way. We had decided not to put the photographs of the true extent of his wounds in any of the media. But of the four big holes in Arthur's back two of them actually had parasites living in them, one in a shell as big as your thumb. Arthur constantly tried to scratch his back, but of course could do nothing about it. We hoped that, given plenty of 'disinfectants' during his time in quarantine, they would heal. And even then, we knew that the problems he had with his teeth, one of his claws and both his ears would need operations at some point soon.

All the time I sat at my desk, dealing with all the post-race work that always seems to arrive in my in-box by the mountain, I found myself worrying about Arthur. I absolutely knew he was in safe hands, and kept telling myself not to worry, but I just hoped he was going to get better. And I hoped that he knew that I would be back to see him soon.

Then, as if my worry had somehow magicked him up out of thin air, I got a message from an adventure racing friend, Johan Hamilton, who worked at an animal hospital in Stockholm. He happened to love dogs, and as a fan of racing he'd actually been one of the first people to become aware of Arthur's story.

And as someone who worked in the veterinary profession, although not a vet himself, he was only too aware of what could be wrong with dogs who hadn't been brought up in the strict care of a Swedish household. He thought Arthur looked a splendid dog, and he loved our story, but he thought he'd almost certainly need proper medical help and check-ups. It was as if he could read our minds.

Johan offered to go out to ScandiPet quarantine centre with one of his veterinary colleagues and examine Arthur to find out what operations he would need when he was finally released from quarantine. His organisation,

Anicura, were prepared to underwrite whatever costs were incurred. It couldn't have been more welcome news.

Although Debbie had said that we shouldn't see Arthur too often we couldn't bear to leave it too long, and planned a visit only two weeks later. We had to see the Peak Performance guys in Stockholm anyway and felt it would be unthinkable not to see Arthur when we would be so near.

While we were making all these plans, I found myself thinking how the media could be such a force for good. After all, it was through the Internet and press stories that Johan had heard about us, and we badly needed his help. And in any case, I knew I could never have done what I did in getting Arthur out of Ecuador without thousands of people supporting me and sending messages of hope and goodwill. It made the most massive difference to me to hear how Arthur's story had affected people all over the world. It made me feel that our story would help not just Arthur, but other people, other animals – and that maybe some of them would be rescued after people read about our story, maybe someone would think twice about mistreating a dog if the story made them start to think that a dog deserved respect and kindness too.

And then it all turned upside down. For whatever motive, no fewer than four people in Ecuador claimed that Arthur belonged to them and that we had 'stolen' him. One of them even gave an interview on Ecuadorian TV. Things were said – by them and in the commentary

– about people from the west dipping into poorer people's lives and taking things away. About people like us not understanding how people in other countries worked. And how we had no right to take Arthur out of the country.

It was painful to read and hear about. Whether their motives were money or fifteen minutes of fame, I didn't know. But I couldn't understand how someone would want to claim that Arthur belonged to them, when he had plainly been at best massively neglected and at worse horribly mistreated. He was dying when we met him. He knew, he must have known, that in the wild he probably only had another six months to live in the condition he was in.

Commentators in Ecuador started to say exactly this. And once the story of these so-called claimants got spread over the Internet there was a terrible backlash, which culminated in a petition to get the man who said Arthur belonged to him prosecuted for cruelty to animals. Thousands of people were signing it, some of them saying some pretty nasty things.

Helena and I found everything about this upsetting. After all, anyone who had followed the story knew that it was Arthur who chose us; he committed himself to us, so we committed ourselves to him. We couldn't leave him to die. So we made a statement on Facebook – which was really all we could do – letting people know that we were against violence of any sort, and that's what we had hoped this story would show people. We were against violence, whether against animals or people, and just wanted to create a debate that might just help mistreated animals. We wanted to *stop* violence, not create it.

It was sad to have our excitement about seeing Arthur marred by all this, but I knew that once I saw him again, he would be the only thing that mattered.

It was soon time to set off for Stockholm and our first visit to ScandiPet. As Helena, Philippa and I sat in the car heading out to there, I started to feel a huge sense of excitement. Soon we would be seeing Arthur again. I couldn't wait to hug him, and for Helena and, very importantly, Philippa, to meet him properly.

Arthur's new temporary home was near beautiful farmland and forest. It was a sunny winter's day when we drew up to the entrance, and it was nice to see Debbie and her local vet standing outside waiting to welcome us.

'He's doing very well,' Debbie said as soon as we got out of the car. 'He's such a super dog. And he seems so calm, so accepting of everything. And he doesn't need too much training. I think he's instinctively a very well-behaved dog.'

We had brought a big new pile of toys for Arthur. I knew that he was a grown-up dog, and that he'd only survived by being mature, independent and calm rather than aggressive or playful. Nevertheless, I thought, a

189

dog's a dog, and they still like to play games, don't they?

But it turned out the only game Arthur wanted to play was to bounce around saying hello.

He was waiting for us in a room at the back of the building; I could hear his familiar woof from behind the door as we got nearer. As soon as Debbie opened the door, it was as if she'd released twenty-seven kilos of fluffy mayhem. Arthur jumped up at me with his tail wagging hard enough to power the local electricity grid.

He put his mouth round my hand as if to say, *Here I am, let's play*. It wasn't like a biting thing, just a playful gesture.

But it made me very aware that I could hardly feel any teeth in his mouth. Although we had always been worried about his teeth, it was only at that moment, when I felt his mouth on my hand, that I fully realised how serious the problem was.

As he started to calm down, and sat at my feet looking up at me and Helena, I wondered again how on earth he could have survived much longer in the Ecuadorian jungle with such damaged teeth.

Philippa meanwhile was watching the proceedings from the safety of her mother's arms. 'Ulv,' she said as she looked sternly at Arthur. She also looked a little bit nervous, but perfectly happy to look at this bouncing furry new member of the family so long as he kept his distance.

'Can we look at his teeth?' I said to Debbie and the vet. 'It's like I can't feel some of them at all.'

We opened Arthur's mouth wide – which he was very good-natured about – and looked at what seemed to be OK teeth at the back. But everything in the front looked damaged or completely worn down.

'He's going to need quite an operation to sort those teeth,' said the vet. 'Maybe he chewed a lot on something hard, like stones, or even a chain he might have been tied up with – it's hard to tell. But they're in a bad way. I'm afraid the more worrying thing is the wounds on his back. Three of them are starting to heal, but the fourth one has something really bad going on deep down. It's not healing, and really we might need to operate and open it all up and see what's going on.'

I looked at Arthur. He seemed so happy and at ease with the world. You would never know he was in such a bad way.

'His ears can be fixed,' the vet went on, 'and we can clip his claws when those sore bits on his paws have healed. His skin's still deeply dirty, but we'll get him properly clean soon.'

It was a long list of things to 'fix', but I was just so happy to see him – and to see that he was so relaxed and happy. And when Helena put Philippa down and let her get a little closer to Arthur, he stayed quite still and very calmly allowed himself to be inspected.

I gave him a bit of a cuddle then, and he got back into his playful mode. There was a table in the corner of the room and as Arthur started bouncing around the place again, he jumped up onto to it, almost from a standing start. It was quite a sight; he was as agile as a cat, and it made me feel happy all over again that he had so much energy. Surely if he could jump about like that then he must have the strength to be able to recover from all the things that were wrong with him.

We took him out into the small yard at the back. I couldn't help looking around at the forests and fields and thinking that Arthur must be missing his 'right to roam'. But he seemed perfectly happy, and anyway, one day – in 106 days, to be precise – he would be running about the fields and forests near us.

After another half an hour of getting to know Arthur, Philippa seemed to be a little bit more relaxed with him. Next time, we decided, we would see if she was happy stroking and patting and playing with him. I felt sure she would be; Arthur seemed to be so gentle with her.

I bent down to say goodbye. I tried to make it a quick cuddle, because I didn't want him to think this was any sort of big goodbye. I would be back soon, and I wanted him – somehow – to know that.

It was painful to shut the door on him and head off towards the car. But he seemed content and was in good hands. And that, for now, was the best we could hope for.

Chapter 12

The Price of Freedom

'If you're bleeding, don't you feel pain?'

Christmas was fast approaching, and though we wouldn't have Arthur with us we wanted to buy him plenty of presents to welcome him to his new home – even if we would have to wait a while before we saw him play with them. Chief among them was a smart shiny, soft, square black bed. We put it in the middle of the floor by the wall in the sitting room. It looked rather as if it had always been there, and we thought that being in the middle of everything was where Arthur would want to be.

To be ready for our second visit, we'd let Philippa choose Arthur's next present – a special sort of dried meat treat. It came in bright pink plastic packaging, which was probably what made Philippa choose it, pink being her very favourite colour. But the long list of healthy things it had in it made me think it was a very good choice for an Arthur present, pink or not.

It would be a busy new year; there were training camps to organise and more sponsors to keep happy. We needed to see Peak Performance again anyway as they had asked us to give all their staff a presentation of the complete Arthur story. And, of course, it was the ideal excuse to go to Manlötens to see how Arthur was getting on and to see if his wounds were healing.

The presentation went like clockwork. I actually enjoy standing up and talking to a room full of people, but sometimes I have an odd moment when I remember how terrified I would have been doing something like that when I was eighteen. But now I find it fun, and I like having the opportunity to tell people about things I am passionate about. And on this occasion, of course, I couldn't have been happier telling them about Arthur.

Some of the talk was a kind of double act with Staffan, but mostly the star of the show was Arthur and all the pictures of him. So by the time we'd finished the talk and the meeting afterwards, I was getting desperate to see the real thing.

All of us – Staffan, Simon, Helena, Philippa and me – set off to ScandiPet as soon as we could. Somehow I felt it was important for Arthur to see 'his' pack again. It wasn't, of course, possible to fly Karen over for the occasion, but otherwise I liked the idea of us being reunited when we weren't all filthy and exhausted.

When we got there, I led the way to the room where I knew Arthur was waiting. Just as before, it was wonderful to see this ball of golden enthusiasm come hurtling towards me. I gave him a huge hug and then got down on the floor and gave him a friendly wrestle. And then, as he went over to be hugged by an enthusiastic Staffan, I got out the brightly packaged meat treat.

Instantly he came rushing back over to me and took the dried meat away from me almost before I had finished unpacking it.

'That was popular,' said Simon, grinning as he watched Arthur sniff and lick his new treat.

'Guess so,' I said, looking at Arthur, now totally focused on the treat. 'Hey boy,' I said to him when he paused in his licking. 'Come here and say a proper hello to Philippa.' I went up to him, but he wasn't having any of it. He was now completely absorbed in getting his back teeth in action on the meat.

I went and sat back in my chair. Arthur had completely ignored me, even when I put out my hand to him and called him by name. I knew perfectly well that you can't really get in between a dog and his food, but this was different. It was as if all his affection as well as his attention was deflected away from me. I found myself feeling, well, 'strange' was how I put it to myself. But moments later, Debbie came into the room and Arthur immediately abandoned the meat and went over to say hello to her, tail wagging.

Somehow these two things made me feel sad. Of course it was wonderful that he was so happy with Debbie, and of course it was great that he appreciated the present we'd so carefully chosen for him. But I'd been waiting for this moment, our few precious moments of our reunion, for ages, and now the whole occasion seemed to be dominated by other things.

Then I told myself not to be ridiculous, and once we started talking with Debbie about the state of Arthur's teeth and wounds, none of these thoughts seemed to matter so much.

Johan had been as good as his word and had been to see Arthur with the chief vet of the Anicura animal hospital in Stockholm. The nice part of his message was that he had fallen for Arthur almost as much as we had. 'He's a very special dog,' Johan had said. 'And he gave me a very special greeting. I think because I am tall and fair, like you, he feels that I must be a good guy and will help him.'

I liked that. I liked the idea that Arthur had a vision of what a good guy looked like, and that guy looked like me.

The less nice news was that the vet had thought the state of his teeth and the wound that hadn't yet healed was very serious. Their official view was also that his teeth were in a terrible state and were causing him some pain, and that an operation was urgently needed on all of these things.

They had left Debbie with lots of advice and antibiotics to try to help with the healing, but felt that Arthur needed to go to the hospital for twenty-four hours to get everything fixed sooner rather than later.

I agreed. 'Whatever it takes,' I said. It was going to be complicated to try to do any of this because Arthur's quarantine meant that strictly speaking he absolutely wasn't allowed to leave Manlötens until 20 March, but I hoped we could persuade the powers that be that it was necessary, as well as safe, given that he'd be going directly to the hospital – with professional vets – and nowhere else.

Whatever happened, Arthur was going to be booked in to Anicura as soon as he was released, but if he needed to be looked at sooner than that then I was determined that nothing and no one would stand in our way.

As we said goodbye to Arthur, trying as before not to make too big a thing of our farewell, I felt that he didn't seem sad enough to see me go. Ridiculous, I told myself again. I'm imagining it. But it was only when he gave me a firm lick on the nose that I managed to convince myself I was being silly.

And yet. This was such a special relationship for me; we had both been through so much, perhaps it wasn't surprising I was sensitive about wanting Arthur to want to be with me above anyone else.

One of my best Christmas presents that year was the final decision by the Swedish Board of Agriculture to allow Arthur out to the animal hospital for his operations. The analysis of his blood and all the other tests showed that he was free of rabies and heartworm (a particularly horrible parasite and one that is apparently quite common in South America), which meant that he wouldn't have to suffer the bad wounds and bad teeth for his last six weeks of quarantine.

He just had to hang on for another couple of weeks or so and then he would have all the help he needed for his wounds, his teeth and his ears. Although we couldn't go and see him to tell him all this, we had regular reports from Debbie, and we were convinced that his operations wouldn't come a moment too soon.

And then towards the end of January, someone at the Swedish Board of Agriculture reversed that decision. I don't think I will ever be able to think kindly of whoever that someone was. The Board had – finally – been responsible for so much happiness by allowing Arthur to leave Ecuador and enter Sweden, and yet now, for no reason that I could make out, they were threatening Arthur's well-being. Despite all the safety procedures we had in place, all the tests and guarantees, Arthur was going to have to bear the septic wound and his terrible teeth and ears for another two months.

Someone there had decided to stick rigidly to the letter of the law. Despite the fact that it was now past the statutory time that had to elapse after the rabies injections, despite the fact that Arthur would not be exposed to anyone except us and the vets, despite the fact that the hospital had set aside an operating slot and told the authorities that all their requirements were met . . . They still would not allow Arthur out of ScandiPet.

Apparently if 'the dog is capable of eating' then his situation couldn't be construed as an emergency.

All the feelings of frustration and despair that I'd had when I was dealing with the authorities in Ecuador came rushing back. It felt like we were back at square one.

Helena, as always, was calm and measured about it all, telling me that if there really was a serious emergency then Debbie's vets could look after him, and he'd be in Anicura's hands before too long anyway.

I wasn't so sure. I became obsessed with the thought that Arthur was in pain and could hardly eat properly with his teeth in such terrible shape. Of the deep festering wounds that he'd had when we first met him one was still dangerous and must, MUST have been painful. 'If you have an open wound,' I said to the Swedish Board of Agriculture, 'don't you think it hurts? If you're bleeding, even if you're a dog, don't you think you feel pain? Just because he can eat something does that mean he's not suffering?'

It was a pretty acrimonious correspondence. But then after two more weeks of my fury and their intransigence, thank goodness – and thanks to Debbie, and probably the treatments from the Anicura vet – the fourth wound opened once again. And this time it started to heal.

Debbie gave me the news over the phone, and of course the first thing I wanted to do was go to Arthur and hug him and make sure he was getting better. But we would have to wait until our next scheduled visit to be able to do that.

There was something else that happened during those weeks to make me feel happy. We found out that Helena was going to have a baby boy. It was early days – he wasn't due until August – but whoever he was going to be, he – like Philippa – could not possibly be more wanted.

I constantly felt I had to pinch myself. For years our family 'unit' had been me and Helena. And now, within months, we would be a family of five. It was an amazing, and wonderful, thought.

All this was happening in the middle of what was an incredibly busy start to our year. The High Coast training camp at the beginning of February was quickly followed by training and teaching in Thailand ready for the next World Series events in the spring. And throughout all of this I was having to get back into shape.

For me getting into shape is rather all or nothing. I am not one of those athletes who makes a point of running upstairs rather than taking the lift, or one who walks everywhere quickly for the sake of it. In fact, most people say I walk as if I were injured. But once I'm in training mode my day is pretty brutal by any normal person's standards.

But that week in February training took a back seat, and we booked a flight to Stockholm to see how Arthur was getting on. By the time we'd hired a car and found somewhere to stay, our visits to Arthur were well on the way to costing us more than the price of several holidays. Not that we were in the slightest bit resentful of that, but as a friend pointed out, Arthur must be close to being the most gold-plated dog in Sweden.

This was rather borne out by the latest news from Johan. Apparently there was really only one surgeon who could do the complicated things for Arthur's teeth that needed doing. He was Danish, world famous, and in such rare demand that he was the only dental vet who has ever given a leopard a gold crown. Anicura was flying him in to Stockholm specially to operate on Arthur.

He was a lucky dog, as well as a gold-plated one.

Friday 20 March 2015 is a date forever etched on my brain and in my heart.

They say that the term 'rollercoaster of emotion' is a bit of a cliché, but there were plenty of times when I couldn't think of any other way of describing those four months of visits to Arthur in quarantine. On the one hand it was so great to see him get better and better, to see his fur get gradually thicker and shinier and his beautiful amber eyes get brighter and brighter. But then on the other hand it was always so sad to say goodbye – even though I tried not to show it, and even though I always tried to make him somehow understand we'd be back soon, it was just awful to shut the door behind us and make our long journey back to Örnsköldsvik.

But finally the day came. We hadn't seen Arthur for more than three weeks, and were all feeling insanely excited at the thought of being able to take him home. As soon as he came out he would be going straight to the hospital for his operations, but he'd be free the next day, free to come home with us for ever.

We arrived in Stockholm the night before his release, and went straight to the hotel where we had a special room booked for him to 'meet the press'. It seemed the whole world wanted to see Arthur on his release, and we were mighty glad to have Lena to help us with the PR of all that.

We were due to pick Arthur up in the morning and then take him straight to Anicura, where we'd also meet up with Staffan. Then after his operation we would come back to the hotel to do press interviews, and on the following day, the Saturday, we had to go on TV to do a live interview. Thank goodness Helena and I were both so excited about the prospect of bringing Arthur home that we didn't have the spare energy to worry about being on live TV. Or not yet, anyway.

Then we'd fly back to Ö'vik the following day, Sunday, the first day of the rest of Arthur's life. We knew the press and TV cameras would follow us there, so – having learned our lesson from last time – we had scheduled the interviews. We had decided we owed it to everyone who wrote to us all the time, and cared about Arthur and his story, to tell them how he was getting on, and to show them a little bit of his new home.

All three of us were up even earlier than usual that morning. Philippa seemed almost as excited as we were, but she'd only met Arthur briefly since her first encounter with him at Stockholm Airport, so Helena was anxious that we were very careful when she met him again properly. We were sure Arthur would be gentle, but he was very big and Philippa was very small, and if she had any sort of fright then she might take a while to get over it.

We set off in the car that was going to take us to Debbie's and told it to go via a special pet shop. It specialised in very smart things for dogs and was the perfect place for us to buy a new lead to celebrate Arthur's new life. We chose a black and gold one that we thought looked suitably regal.

As we got into the car, my phone buzzed. Debbie. For a second I felt my heart skip a beat. Was something wrong? Was Arthur OK? Surely he couldn't have any new problem with the wound, or his teeth, could he?

'What's wrong?' I said, sounding a little bit hysterical even to my ears. 'Is Arthur OK?'

'No, he's fine, don't worry,' said Debbie. 'We're all ready for you. You'll be here in an hour, yes? But it's very odd,' she went on. 'All this morning Arthur's been bouncing around like mad. It's as if he knows that today's the day. I think he'll be so happy to see you.'

'That's so great,' I said. 'Just great. See you in about an hour.'

As I disconnected I thought how sad she'd sounded. She'd loved having Arthur, and I knew it was going to be a wrench for her to say goodbye. What an amazing presence his is, I thought for the hundredth time. He affects everyone he comes across. In a good way. Even someone who dealt with dogs all the time, like Debbie, knew straight away how special he was.

We drew up to ScandiPet less than an hour later. I'd been so pleased to hear that Arthur seemed to sense we were coming to get him. After that odd moment last time when I thought he was more interested in the meat I had brought him than he was in me, and that moment of jealousy I had felt at the way he'd bounded up to Debbie, I had realised I had a strange capacity to be hurt by Arthur. Almost like a love affair.

And yet, I knew I never really doubted him, any more than he doubted me.

The three of us climbed out of the car. Helena and Philippa looked like two peas in a pod, in their mother–daughter trademark pink Puffas. I took a moment out of my excitement and preoccupation with Arthur to think how great they looked.

Helena was holding Philippa's hand firmly as we went to the entrance, where we could see Debbie waiting for us. As we got nearer we could hear the familiar deep bark. Arthur *did* sound so excited.

We went into his bit of yard, and there he was. He seemed to bounce ten feet in the air as I got near. Jumping up at me, trying to lick my face in mid-air. I was just as crazy. I couldn't hug him enough. He put his mouth round my hands in his usual playful way but this time he seemed almost beside himself with excitement.

Helena and Debbie looked on with smiles on their faces. Eventually Arthur calmed down a bit, and so did I. We told Philippa to come and say a proper hello. She did look small in her big pink coat as she approached him. And nervous.

Arthur, though, was now quite calm and was very happy to be given a hug by Helena. Gently Helena took Philippa's hand and put it on the back of Arthur's head. Still a bit nervous, Philippa gave him a hesitant stroke.

'That's it,' said Helena. 'See how gentle he is. If you're gentle with him he'll be gentle back.'

Arthur was looking at both of them with a completely calm expression. As Debbie said, he seemed totally accepting of everything, and I knew then that I'd been right; he'd never in a million years do anything to hurt Philippa. Even if he wasn't already the gentlest dog in the world, he knew she was with me, and anyone who was with me was all right by him.

I'd already decided that the first thing Arthur and I were going to do together was go for his first freedom run. He'd spent weeks and weeks looking out of the quarantine yard at the forest beyond, and I wanted to take him there just so he could see what it was really like.

I put his smart new lead on him and told everyone that we'd be just ten minutes, but that I needed to do this.

As we set off over the wintry leaves lying on the ground towards the trees in the distance Arthur jumped up at me constantly, trying to reach my hand, trying to play even as we were running. I now knew that this was his way of talking to me. His way of saying, *This is all I ever wanted.*

I let him off his smart new lead – I knew he wasn't going anywhere – and ran on a bit further. I didn't want to go back to everyone else just yet. Apart from anything else, there were tears pouring down my face and I knew there were more where they came from.

Arthur and I came back across the crackling, frosty ground and went up to where Helena, Philippa and the others were standing. Johan and the vet from Anicura had now arrived ready to take us to the clinic, so we would be quite a crowd arriving for Arthur's operation.

'Time to go now,' I said to everyone, still feeling very emotional, but finished with crying for the moment. I led the way back over to the cars.

We had just started to load up all Arthur's things – it was amazing how much stuff he seemed to have accumulated while he was in quarantine – when I realised that Debbie had disappeared. I went back into the building and headed towards the offices, where Debbie was putting some papers away.

'Aren't you coming out to say goodbye?' I asked her. She looked up and I could see tears in her eyes.

'I could introduce you to one of the vets who's going to do the operation. He's just arrived,' I said.

Debbie put the pile of papers she was holding down on the desk, went round the other side and sat down. She looked down at the files for a moment and then looked up and said, 'No, Mikael, I won't come and say goodbye. I know he'll be all right now. I'm just glad we were able to help.'

Her eyes were shining with unshed tears.

We looked at each other and smiled. We didn't really have to spell it out to each other: we had both been touched for ever by Arthur and we didn't have to say that out loud.

Arthur got into the front of the car with me, and sat in the footwell by my feet. He seemed totally unsurprised by everything, obviously content just to be sitting quietly in the same space as me. As I looked down at his shiny fur and his back, now nearly free of wounds and scars, I thought of the last time I'd looked down on him like this, on that long journey from Mompiche to Quito. How different things had seemed then, with only the ghost of a hope of our being together – and yet now here we were, only two days away from actually going home.

When our little cortège carrying Arthur arrived at the vet clinic, I guess we shouldn't have been surprised to find the ranks of cameras and press outside. But still it took me by surprise that so many people were interested enough to be at an animal hospital first thing in the morning.

As ever, Arthur seemed to take it all in his stride, looking eagerly and calmly about him. Then when he saw Staffan he bounced up to him and woofed happily as Staffan gave him a big hug.

We made our way to the waiting room to do the media things we had to do before Arthur had his operation. We had committed to give two interviews to Swedish TV, and then I had to do radio down-the-line interviews and another interview for Aftonbladet TV.

I answered everyone's questions with Arthur sitting quietly by my feet. Every interviewer and every cameraman went up to Arthur to say hello and give him a welcome pat. And to everyone Arthur seemed to be faultlessly polite. Yet again, I thought what a grown-up, calm attitude he had to life – all these people and noise and lights and yet nothing seemed to ruffle him.

Instead it was me who was nervous and on edge – not with the interviewers, I was fast becoming used to that, but with the thought that Arthur was going to have such a big operation.

Of course it was wonderful that we had Scandinavia's – if not the world's – best dental vet operating, but Arthur was going to have a long anaesthetic because of all the operations on his ears and claws as well as his teeth. It was hard not to dwell on all the serious things that were going to be done to him.

I left Arthur with Johan, Staffan and Helena and all the press people and went off to do the radio interview in a quiet room at the back of the hospital. Lena showed me into the room and left me to it.

It was national radio so I was concentrating hard on getting everything right, and making sure that I acknowledged by name everyone who had been so helpful to us. So it took me a while to realise that the door had opened and Lena was standing there looking anxiously at me.

Thinking I was saying something wrong, I frowned up at her, but she just shook her head. I was so on edge that I cut the radio interview short, disconnected the line and asked her what was wrong.

'You're wanted in the waiting room,' she said. 'It's Arthur. He's got very upset.'

I put down the phone and followed her out of the room as quickly as I could. As I got to the waiting room, I could hear barking and howling, and scratching noises coming from the door. Arthur.

I opened the door, and had just about enough time to take in the banks of worried-looking faces that lined the walls of the small waiting room. But then Arthur jumped up at me as he saw me, gave another bark and a bit of a whimper and seemed to calm down.

I made a lot of fuss of him, and he seemed to be relaxed and calm again as we went over and joined the others.

'He went pretty crazy as soon as you left the room,' said Johan. 'Just scratching at the door, and rushing about in circles.'

'It's all very strange for him,' said Helena. 'I think he's calm really, but he doesn't like it if you're not here.'

By now Arthur was lying quietly by my side, as if nothing much had happened. I decided not to worry about anything except his forthcoming operation.

Moments later two nurses and the vet came to take him away. Perhaps, I thought as they led him out of the door, he knew what was going to happen and had got anxious, or perhaps he could feel my anxiety.

'Come on,' said Helena sensibly. 'Let's go and get something to eat. He's in good hands now, and there's nothing more we can do. We've just got to wait.' She looked at me, concerned. 'And try not to worry,' she added.

Of course, and as Helena knew very well, trying 'not to worry' was easier said than done. The next few hours passed unbelievably slowly. And although the staff put their heads round the door from time to time to say all was well, nothing and nobody could stop me being rigid with tension.

I was curled up on a chair in the corner of the room when another knock on the door interrupted our attempts to talk about something else. It was the hospital vet. He looked very worried. So worried that my heart sank, and I could hardly get the words out as I tried to ask him what the matter was.

'Mikael,' he said. 'We need you to come. We need you to come and help.'

'What? Why?' I stuttered incoherently. 'Me?'

'Yes,' said the vet. 'You. I think only you can do this.'

'But I don't understand,' I said. 'I'm not a vet. I'm not a doctor. What can I do? I'm not a professional. You're the professionals.' I felt utterly confused. If they couldn't fix things, then what hope did I have?

And anyway, what *was* wrong?

'I think you'd better come with me,' the vet said. 'You'll see.'

I looked at Helena, who was looking just as worried as I felt. I turned and followed the vet out of the waiting room.

As we walked along the passages towards the operating theatre at the back of the building I started to hear a terrible howling. It was like nothing I'd ever heard before.

Like a creature in unimaginable pain. Pain and utter misery. As I got nearer to a door at the end of the corridor it got louder and louder. It was almost unbearable.

'What on *earth*?' I said to the vet.

'I know,' he said. 'Arthur's come out of the anaesthetic, and he's in that recovery room. We can't do anything with him; he's been like that ever since he came round. I've never come across anything quite like it.' He opened the door to a small room that looked like an outsize shower cubicle.

In the middle of it, lying in a sort of metal cot, was Arthur. He had his eyes shut and his mouth wide open, emitting this terrible, terrible high-pitched howl of misery.

I felt the tears prick my eyes. Had I done this to him? Was this my fault? Had I somehow been responsible for causing all this harm and pain to Arthur, who I only ever wanted to look after? I fell to my knees and put my arms round him, trying to transmit some sort of comfort to his trembling body.

As soon as he felt my touch he opened his eyes, and seemed to breathe out. The terrible noise stopped instantly, as if my putting my arms round him had flicked a switch. He seemed to relax, and let out a little whimper and shut his eyes again.

I held him close. It was the most unexpected and extraordinary sensation. I could feel that he was all right now. I could feel that he was now Arthur again. Traumatised but no longer desperate.

'Hey boy,' I said into his shoulder as I held him close. 'All right now, boy. All right now.'

I got down on the floor so that I was as close to him as I could possibly be. I put my head next to his and looked into his eyes as he opened them again. He just gave a small snuffle and tried to get his head even nearer to mine. I put my arms round him.

We stayed like that for a long time.

Chapter 13

Acute Separation Anxiety

'I don't know if we can do this . . .'

I guess the vets at Anicura had started to find the silence almost as disturbing as Arthur's howling, because after a while there was a tentative knock on the door of the recovery room.

'Everything OK?' said one of the nurses.

'Yes,' I said, looking at Arthur who had just closed his eyes again – but this time in a peaceful way. 'Yes, we're fine. Coming out now.'

I opened the door. Arthur got to his feet with what seemed like a rather sleepy scramble. But it was clear he was absolutely determined not to let me out of his sight.

The vet was standing in the background. 'Might be an idea to take him out into the yard at the back. Give him some space and some air.'

He handed me one of the clinic's leads, which I clipped round Arthur as we went out of the door at the back of the building. The vet came with me and watched as Arthur trotted behind me.

'You know,' she said, 'that's something quite extraordinary you have there. Your relationship with him, I mean. I've been working with dogs – and people – for years and years and I think I've only ever once come across a bond as deep as you have with Arthur.'

I looked at Arthur. And then I bent down, and scratched the place behind his ear that he liked having scratched. I could see that his ear was now clean and mended and what had looked like a deep black infection was now glowing pink.

'I think,' I said as I stroked Arthur's golden head, 'that maybe it's to do with meeting in extreme circumstances. You know, like sweethearts in the war who only meet for one day and then five years later when the war's over they take up where they left off because the relationship was always there. Something about being in danger, meeting briefly, making things so much more intense.'

I'm no psychologist, but I did know that what I had with Arthur was special. And now, after what had just happened, I knew that our bond was every bit as strong as I had thought it was.

It was late afternoon now, and time to go back to the hotel to introduce the newly mended Arthur to the press and his well-wishers. Helena, Staffan, Philippa and I got into the lead car to head off to the Clarion Collection Hotel Tapto where we were due to have the interviews. They'd also laid on a special dog room for Arthur to spend the night. I loved the fact that Sweden was wheeling out such a good welcome for Arthur's first day of liberty.

We all settled down in the big interview room. Arthur was quite quiet now, which I guess wasn't surprising as he'd been under anaesthetic for a long time. As the teams of journalists and photographers trooped in he sat, subdued, in the corner.

By now, it was becoming very familiar to me to talk about Arthur and my joy at his release and his returning health. I looked at my friend Staffan, and at Helena, as I was talking, and could see how jubilant they were too that this day had finally come.

I was *almost* entirely happy to talk to the press about being happy. But not quite entirely. Halfway through the sessions, Arthur, whose insides had obviously been upset by the trauma he'd gone through, had a quiet dump in the corner of the room. Anyone could see that he was distressed by it – we knew from Debbie and what we'd seen that he never pooped or peed indoors – so I hated having to see a journalist take photos of it and home in on it to make a story.

It was, though, the only sour moment of the day. In every other way everyone was joining me in my delight on this, the first day of Arthur being a free member of our family.

When the interviews finally came to an end we headed off to the rooms the hotel had allocated us. We'd decided that Staffan and I would be in the 'dog room' with Arthur, leaving Helena and Philippa to sleep peacefully in the main room.

As we sat around our room having snacks from room service, I looked at Philippa looking at Arthur. So far so good, I thought. She seemed a bit wary, but also fascinated by this big furry creature lying on the floor. 'Ulv,' she said again, pointing at him. I knew he'd be 'Arthur' to her soon enough, but for now I rather liked her name for him.

We were all pretty shattered by the day, and were due at the TV studios very early the following morning, so we all went to sleep in our allotted rooms ridiculously early.

Seven hours later and I had probably managed about the same amount of sleep as I might get during a race.

Arthur's insides were clearly still very upset, and he had bad diarrhoea. But being a very clean dog, he knew he had to go outside every time he had to go. With the result that I had to take him outside pretty well every half an hour throughout the night. Poor Arthur, I thought, but I did hope he was going to get better. I didn't fancy having to take him outside all through the night for years.

But it was soon time to worry about something entirely different – the live national morning show on TV4. We arrived at the studios in time for make-up at 8 a.m., and were shown round the set. We were going to be sitting on high stools opposite the interviewer, and in the background there were lights, chairs and a sort of kitchen where someone would be preparing a meal for Arthur while we were talking. It was a weird combination of the real and unreal.

In another life, Arthur must have been some sort of movie star, because once again the cameras and lights didn't seem to bother him at all. It also seemed as if his insides were settling down, as we hadn't had to rush him outside before we left the hotel or after we arrived at the studios.

The interview itself went incredibly smoothly. They said that Helena and I talked as if we were sitting in our own home. Which I suppose is how it should be on a show like that. And I found that, as usual, I was just happy talking about Arthur, and the fact that he was sitting on the floor beside us just made it all the happier.

Still with our make-up on, we left the studio to get back to the hotel. We had some free time, so I decided we should take Arthur for a bit of a walk. The streets around the hotel were very quiet, and there was a small grassy area where it might be possible to let Arthur run about a bit. I thought perhaps fresh air and exercise would be good for his insides and make him feel better again.

We set off – Helena, Staffan and me, with Philippa in the buggy – and walked around for about half an hour. Arthur seemed happy to walk next to Philippa's buggy, and didn't pull on his lead or seem to want to rush off and look for interesting smells. Maybe he was still subdued by his operation, but he behaved so quietly and beautifully that it seemed as if he'd gone for walks on a lead on the pavements of capital cities all his life.

It was time for Philippa to have her lunch, so we left her and Helena to go back to the big room with Arthur.

Staffan and I wanted to go to the hotel gym and do some serious interval training. We only had a couple of weeks until a big Series race in Chile, so we rather needed to get our training in when we could.

I bent down to the buggy and kissed Philippa on the cheek as she got in the lift with Helena and Arthur. It was great to see the three of them so calm in each other's company.

Ten minutes into our training and I became aware of my phone buzzing from the corner of the gym. I stopped the treadmill session I'd started and went over to pick up. It was Helena.

'Not good here,' she said. 'Arthur's in a very bad way – listen to him howl.' And yes, I could hear him howl. It was a low-pitched whine, like a wolf might make. 'I'm going to take him out of the room and bring him down to the lobby, but you need to come,' she said.

Bathed in sweat, I headed out of the gym and went down to the lobby. Helena was sitting there looking tense and worried, with Philippa in the buggy and Arthur sitting by her side. When he saw me he quickly trotted up to me, and didn't take his eyes off me as I went over to Helena and Philippa.

'He's just been sitting here, waiting, waiting,' said Helena. 'He was terrible up there in the room.' She looked quite shaken. 'I know. Hard to believe now because he's just so happy you're here. But if he's going to do this every time he's separated from you, well, I don't know what we're going to do.'

I sat down next to Helena. Arthur came and sat by my foot, still not taking his eyes off me.

'OK,' I said. 'Let's go up to the room now. Let's get Philippa used to him being quieter.'

We went back up to the room with Staffan, and settled down to order some food and to just be together and try to make Arthur get used to all of us – together or separately.

As soon as we got to the room Arthur flopped down on the floor and lay there quite quietly. It was difficult to believe he had been so frighteningly agitated, but I could see he was still not himself. He was lying on his side, not on his front as he'd mostly done when we'd visited him in quarantine and when he was with us in Mompiche.

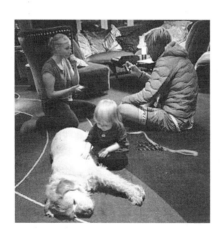

But now he seemed so calm that even Philippa thought it was safe to approach. She got on her knees and edged over towards him, and then put her hand on his side in an exploring, tentative way. Arthur, though wide awake, didn't react. So Philippa started stroking his side and inspecting his thick gold fur at close quarters.

At that moment all I could think was how lovely they looked – Arthur now quite still and relaxed, and Philippa being friendly and getting more confident.

I took a quiet picture of them both, and thought, *It's going to be all right after all.*

The next morning was a flurry of a different sort of activity. Lena was helping us again with all the media who'd be at Stockholm Airport when we left and when we landed at Örnsköldsvik, and she had set up a schedule for a limited number of press people – the ones who had been so supportive of my mission to bring Arthur to Sweden – to see him and us at home.

There would be some interviews the following day too, but we were firm that no one was to be allowed inside or near the house when Arthur first arrived. He must have calm while he inspected his new home.

We rushed around getting our things together, packing up the cars ready to go to the airport. Arthur came and sat in the passenger seat at the back with me. We knew he would have to go in his kennel as soon as we checked in for the flight, but we wanted to put off that moment for as long as possible.

Stockholm's Arlanda Airport is a massive international hub, which some people find overwhelming and confusing. Not so the Swedish media, who seemed to know exactly where and when we'd have to go for our local Höga Kusten flight to Örnsköldsvik. As we drew up at one end of Terminal 4, there they were in huge numbers, flashing cameras at the ready.

Arthur had his smart 'Welcome Home' lead on that I'd bought him for the day of his release from quarantine, but he didn't need any lead because he stuck by me like glue as the photographers and journalists crowded round. He seemed to have recovered from his stomach upset too, and was taking all the attention in his stride as usual.

Even when we brought out his special blue travelling kennel he seemed relatively unruffled, and allowed us to put him in and close the door without making any sort of fuss.

The plane we were travelling on was a much smaller plane than the jumbos he'd flown on so far. It was propeller driven and only took about sixty passengers. Apparently one of the passengers on our flight that Sunday was allergic to dogs, so there was no question of having Arthur in the passenger area of the cabin with us. But at least he could have his kennel up at the front of the plane with some other cargo, separated from us by rope netting. At least he wasn't going to be in the hold.

We said our last goodbyes to Staffan, who was catching a different plane, and to the Stockholm press. We knew there would be more press when we landed at Ö'vik, but it would be nice to have a couple of hours of calm on the plane before it all started again.

At least that's what I thought.

Helena, Philippa and I followed Arthur's kennel up the steps and watched the steward put it behind the rope netting, at the front of the plane just behind the cockpit. And then we went through to take our seats. Everyone on the plane knew we had the precious cargo of Arthur on board and as we walked down the gangway many of them smiled and nodded at us.

Looking at the warm, friendly faces around me, I thought once again how great it was that Arthur's story seemed to make people so happy.

And then it started.

The doors were still open and there was a cold wind blowing through the plane. The engines were ticking over, the heaters were humming and there was a murmur of conversation on the plane. But then moments later, there was no noise that could have drowned the sound coming from the roped-off area at the front of the plane.

It was like the dreadful high-pitched scream of pain that had been so terrible to hear in the clinic.

Arthur was howling and howling, seemingly without drawing breath. It was truly awful to hear. The people on the plane around me couldn't disguise their horror. I couldn't blame them, since it sounded like nothing so much as a creature being horribly tortured.

A stewardess came down the gangway towards me, grimacing at the piercing noise. 'I'm sorry sir,' she said, 'but the captain says that he cannot fly the plane with this going on. I think somehow you must calm your dog down.'

I followed her to the front of the plane. Ahead of me I could see through the door of the cockpit the pilot and co-pilot turning round in their seats, looking at me with expressions of concern.

The stewardess held the rope netting aside so I could get behind and kneel down by the kennel. As soon as Arthur saw me his terrible howling stopped. He looked at me with his trusting amber eyes, but I thought I could detect a look of hurt. As if to say, *Why are you doing this to me? What's going on? Where have you been?*

'Hey, boy,' I said as I put my fingers between the mesh of the kennel door. 'Hey Arthur. It won't be long. You're safe, but you've got to stay in your kennel.'

Arthur licked my fingers but still seemed to be disorientated. The chill air continued to roar through the cargo area; I was sure a cold wind wasn't helping him get used to being where he was.

Then I thought perhaps it would help if he had a bit of me, like he had in the van in Quito. Quickly I whipped off my jersey and took off the T-shirt underneath. (I was pretty sure no one would object to a moment of half-naked adventure racer if it was for a good cause.) I quickly opened the kennel door and put the T-shirt next to Arthur. He started sniffing it immediately.

I looked up at the stewardess. 'I think he'll start howling again if I go back to my seat. Can I stay here?'

'No,' she said, although I could tell she felt very sorry for Arthur. 'We're going to close the doors now ready for take-off and you must go back to your seat, but then when we reach 30,000 feet the captain says you can come forward and be with Arthur.'

I let Arthur have one last lick of my fingers, and then as the 'doors to automatic' instruction came over the speakers went back to my seat. Helena, with Philippa sitting calmly by her side, looked up as I came back.

'He doesn't like being shut up in a cold noisy plane, does he?' she said. 'He's going to start again in a moment.'

And sure enough, as the engines revved up for take-off and the seatbelt signs went on the terrible noise started up again. Helena and I just looked at each other, and made apologetic faces to the other passengers for the few minutes it took to reach the right height. The noise of Arthur's howling was no less terrible, but at least I knew I would be able to comfort him soon.

The stewardess headed our way as soon as the seatbelt signs went off. 'You can go to the front now,' she said. 'And the sooner the better,' she added with a smile.

I made my way to the cargo area as quickly as I could. As I bent down to the kennel's entrance Arthur took one look at me and immediately went quiet.

'OK, Arthur?' I said. 'OK now?' I pushed my fingers through the mesh, and sat down.

The flight was only going to be an hour or so, but I knew where I had to be for every minute of it.

It was strange to arrive back at Ö'vik Airport with a new member of the family. The tiny airport had thirty or more journalists waiting by the luggage belt, which made the small waiting area look very full. And by the time the other passengers emerged and our luggage started to come out there was a sort of chaos.

And then everything got even more chaotic, as two grinning baggage handlers came through the staff door carrying Arthur's kennel.

A cheer went up from the crowd and the press, and everyone started smiling again. 'Welcome home, Arthur,' several people cried out as I opened the kennel door.

Arthur came out quite calmly, gave himself a bit of a shake and looked around incuriously at the crowd, and then trustingly at me. It was as if he had never had those moments of panic and anguish on the plane.

I clipped his best lead on him and took him to the airport entrance to talk to some of the press and show him the light dusting of snow that had showered Ö'vik that morning.

Some of the press were coming to have a formal interview the following day, but for now it was time to head home, to introduce Arthur to his bed and his house, and to hope that he liked it as much as we did.

Chapter 14

Coming Home

'. . . but what if he doesn't like it?'

As we drove the twenty minutes or so from the airport to home, I looked around at the lakes and forests and small villages on the way, all covered in a sprinkling of picturesque snow. I tried to look at the scenery from Arthur's point of view. There, I thought, was the kind of trail he might like to run up, and there, a lake that he might like to cool himself in on a hot day. I wondered what he'd make of the snow – not just the light dusting we had now, but the deep snowdrifts we would have in the depths of winter. And I hoped he'd be able to orientate himself soon, and never ever get lost.

Arthur was sitting in the footwell on the passenger side of the car; he seemed to be just as happy there as he had been on his other car journeys. I thought we should probably get him used to being in the back of the car in future, but for now I wanted him to be as near to me as possible.

As we came up the main road towards the turn-off to our house, I found myself hoping and hoping that he would like what he found. This was for good; this was our future together, the future for all of us. For me, for him and Helena, Philippa and the new arrival, our baby boy due in August. And yet it couldn't be more different to the place he'd come from. I *did* hope he would like what he found.

I must have looked as tense as I felt, because Helena – sitting in the back with Philippa – leaned forward and said, 'Hey, don't worry. I'm sure he'll love it. After all, it's where you are, so it's got to be all right, hasn't it?'

I hoped she was right.

We drew up to the front of the house. The lights were on and it looked very welcoming on a grey afternoon.

'OK,' I said as we parked the car and Helena gathered a sleepy Philippa into her arms. 'This is it.'

I went round to the other side of the car and opened the door. Arthur jumped out and immediately started sniffing the wheels of the car, the grass at the front of the house and the two snow-clad canoes that were lying against the wall. I followed him around as he made his inspections, holding his lead loosely even though I knew he wasn't going anywhere. Helena started to unload the car, and together we carried Philippa and the piles of luggage into the house.

We had left everything tidy, but not too tidy, just like it would be on a normal day, with Arthur's black shiny bed in its place in the sitting room and two new bowls, one for his water and one for his food, in the kitchen. And we had left all the doors open upstairs and downstairs so that Arthur could explore the whole house as soon as he arrived. We put everything down by the front door and I bent down to take off his lead.

As soon as he was free, Arthur trotted forward into the sitting room. He sniffed the sofa, the chairs, and all the corners of the kitchen. Then he came back to his bed and stood in the middle of it and started scratching and pawing at it, turning round as he did so. Then he flopped down in the middle of it and looked about him.

'Well, that's promising,' said Helena. 'He seems to know that's his bed.'

Then Arthur, knowing his work wasn't yet done, got up again and resumed his sniffing inspection. He went out into the garden room at the side of the sitting room, sniffed the garden tools lying by the outside door, and then came trotting back to the hall and went straight up the stairs.

I picked up Philippa, by now very sleepy indeed, and together with Helena went upstairs after Arthur. First he went into our room and sniffed the duvet, the cupboard and all the bits of floor round the edges, then he went into Philippa's room and checked out the bed, her box of toys and the smell of the curtains. Seeming to be satisfied with all that, he then went into our office, checked all the filing cabinets, the leads for the computers and the pile of training shoes in the corner. Finally he went into the room with the treadmill, the weights and the equipment boxes to have a sniff around there.

And then, as if to say, *That's all fine*, he went downstairs, had a quick sniff of the front door and the laundry room next to it and went back to his new bed.

'Isn't that great?' I said, knowing there was a goofy smile on my face. 'I think home has passed the Arthur Test.'

'I think,' said Helena, smiling too, 'that he likes it because it smells of you.'

Philippa was awake now, and it was time for a walk. We thought it would be good if Helena took Arthur with Philippa in the buggy and see what happened. After all the worry of Arthur's howling in Stockholm we knew he had to get used to the idea that I wouldn't always be with him.

I helped them get ready, and then went back into the house to deal with unpacking and all the calls I had to return and emails to send – the following day was going to be a busy one.

When I got up to the office I looked out of the window to see how they were getting on. Helena, pushing the buggy, was halfway down the road, and Arthur was walking by her side, not pulling on the lead at all. He seemed to be just as calm as the time we all went for a walk in Stockholm.

They came back just as I finished a long conversation with Swedish TV. 'He was fine,' said Helena, smiling as she unclipped Arthur's lead. 'I think it's going to be OK.'

'Perfect,' I said. 'And now it's time for his first supper in his new home.'

I had filled up Arthur's water bowl, and I had prepared his very own special meatballs in the other bowl. I had made sure they were exactly the same kind that I had given him that unforgettable time in Ecuador, the same flavour, the same size and I had even heated them up in the thermal sleeve.

Arthur trotted into the kitchen and headed straight for

the water bowl. It was lovely to hear that ferocious slurping noise in our kitchen.

Then he turned to the bowl of meatballs. He had a bit of a sniff, and then turned round and went back to his bed.

Incredible! So much for my magic meatball moment. 'Arthur,' I said. 'What's the matter? Aren't you hungry?'

Arthur got up and came over to the bowl. He gave the meatballs a lick, and then started to eat them.

Perhaps his dental operations had left him with different taste buds, or perhaps he only wanted to eat things if it was clear that I was going to eat them too. Either way, I could see there were going to be lots of things we were going to have to find out about each other.

As we were all going to have an early start the following day, and as we were all a bit drained from the last four days, we decided to put everybody to bed early. Arthur was now flopped by the front door, so I thought I'd take him outside to see if he'd perform in the woods behind our house. I knew his insides were still not quite right, but I hoped that his quarantine training and his instincts, and his realisation that here was home, would mean that there wouldn't be any question of his pooping on his own doorstep. Or, more to the point, inside it.

It was nearly dark when we set off, but still possible to see where we were going. Holding Arthur's lead, I picked up speed and ran towards the woods. Arthur bounded along beside me and then drew to a halt.

He settled down to do his business. Good, I thought. When he was finished he then dug like crazy with his front paws to bring earth up to cover what he'd done. He was amazingly diligent. I'd only ever seen dogs give the most cursory kick with their back legs to cover their poop, but Arthur went for it like his life depended on it, and really did cover up what he'd done with a pile of earth. Perhaps, I thought, over on the other side of the world, his life really *had* depended on his covering his tracks.

We jogged back together, untroubled by any people or dogs, and I thought again what an enormous contrast this new life of his was going to be. No threats, just loving kindness.

When we got back, Arthur seemed to know exactly what to do and headed straight for his bed. With a scramble and a scratch and a couple of complete revolutions, he flopped down and closed his eyes.

'Sleep well, Arthur,' I said softly. 'Welcome home.'

I woke up as soon as it was light. For a split second I felt disorientated. Something was different. And then the next second I knew what it was: Arthur was downstairs.

At least I hoped he was.

I got up and went downstairs as quickly as I could. There, looking as if he had been sleeping there all his life, was Arthur in the middle of his bed, head on his front paws, looking sleepy. He looked as if he hadn't stirred all night. He raised his head as I came over to him, and began to wag his big golden tail. As if to say, *I'm all right down here, but it's nice to see you.* I cupped his head in my hands and gave him a quick kiss on his nose. Time for a run, I thought, before the media mayhem begins.

Arthur got up and went over to his water bowl. He quickly slurped the water that I'd left him the night before and then padded over to the front door, looked at me and then looked back at the door. It was clear what he wanted.

I clipped on his lead and together we set off for our second walk in the woods. Just as he had the previous evening, he trotted by my side, exactly in step with me, and then suddenly halted, lifted his leg and relieved himself against a tree. He then went through the vigorous digging and covering up routine that he'd used before.

By the time we got back to the other side of the woods, he had done this five more times, and every time he'd dug hard and long into the earth to cover them. I realised this was very much part of Arthur; he would take as long as it took. But otherwise, I thought, as we bounced along on the leafy ground, he was a wonderfully thoughtful companion. Running at my pace and not pulling or trying to run off.

As we turned the corner of the last path before the home run back to the house, a walker came towards us from the top of the path. I could see that behind him there was a big boisterous-looking dog of a breed I couldn't identify. He was black and brown and started barking as soon as he caught sight of Arthur. He came bounding up to us, and danced around Arthur growling and darting, with teeth bared.

I didn't know the dog or the owner, and suddenly wondered what the dog-owner protocol was if your dog unwittingly got into a fight and one or other of them was badly injured. This particular dog was almost as big as Arthur and seemed – to me at least – rather vicious.

The owner was shouting at him to come away, but his dog was completely ignoring him; the more he was shouted at the louder he barked and the more he bared his teeth.

I started to worry for Arthur, so new to everything, and still recovering from all the trauma of his operations. But in fact the only one of us who remained totally serene was Arthur himself. He barged his way past the other dog – just pushed him out of the way – and carried on trotting in the direction of home.

The other dog, looking a bit puzzled, stopped barking and turned round as if to say, *Whatever, I didn't want a fight anyway.* His owner and I briefly exchanged glances. No harm done. And we went on our way.

As I watched Arthur calmly trotting ahead of me, with just the right tension on the lead, I thought I had probably just seen one of the secrets of Arthur's survival. He was big enough and mature enough not to get into fights; he had street skills.

I wondered, yet again, what could have damaged his back so badly. After what I'd just witnessed, I thought it seemed unlikely to have been caused by another dog. Maybe it was inflicted by a human, maybe by some piece of machinery he had somehow got trapped in. We would never know.

But one thing was for sure: nothing like that would ever happen to him again so long as I was around.

As Arthur and I rounded the corner to home I could see that the TV crews and radio vans were already filling up the road. There were people wherever you looked, bristling with sound booms, aerials and cameras. Happily our neighbours had been following our story with almost as much excitement as the media, so I hoped they wouldn't mind the neighbourhood being dominated by journalists and their technology.

It took a while to actually get back inside the house because, as ever, there seemed to be so many people who wanted to say hello to Arthur and welcome him to Sweden.

Saying hello to Arthur always seemed to take a long time, with everyone wanting at least a pat and a word, if not a whole conversation. But soon we were back to film-ing – with Arthur the relaxed TV star that he now always seemed to be.

The TV people wanted pictures of Arthur and Philippa together – as I rather thought they would – and it was lovely to watch Arthur be so contented in the middle of so much fuss.

At one point he was lying on his side in the middle of the floor, and Philippa was lying on him, as if his stomach was an extra-thick furry pillow. She had her arms round him and was smiling cheerfully for the cameras. Arthur just lay there with his eyes half closed as if nothing at all were happening.

For most of the day Helena and I sat at our dining room table happily answering endless questions from the interviewers. This really was the acceptable face of the media; everyone just seemed so happy for us, no detail of our first day with Arthur home seemed too small for them to ask us about.

When we finally broke for lunch we gave Arthur a special bone as a bit of a reward for being so patient. He had just started to get thoroughly into it, chewing hard on one end of it and holding it firmly in his front paws, when I saw Philippa come up to him, bend down and start to pull the bone out of his grasp.

Alarmed, I leapt up to stop her. After all, a dog whose every piece of food must have been so hard-earned was surely likely to get angry if it was suddenly taken away from him.

But to my amazement, Arthur just let go, put his head back on his paws and half closed his eyes. Philippa stood up and waved the bone triumphantly up in the air, as if she'd fought long and hard for it.

'That's so great,' said Helena, who had been watching with some concern too. 'He seems absolutely cool with kids, doesn't he?'

There was time before the next interview to go for another run with Arthur. Leaving Helena with Lena and all the journalists, I clipped on Arthur's lead and we set off towards the woods.

We crossed the road and trotted up the hill towards the school and some houses. In the middle of the houses was an entrance to a trail that led through the woods; this was almost certainly going to be one of Arthur's regular walks.

Together we ran through the trail in the woods, three or four times meeting other dogs and their owners. The owners stopped with a cry of 'Arthur!', and some of them wanted to say a proper hello to him, which was great. We sped on through and out of the woods, Arthur keeping perfect pace beside me and not at all perturbed by the smatterings of snow on the paths.

We headed back down the hill, and turned off to our road. I was just slowing down when suddenly the lead was jerked hard and unceremoniously out of my hand. I had got so used to Arthur being by my side that I wasn't holding the lead very tightly, so I could only watch in horror as Arthur shot across the road, made straight for the house at the end of the row and disappeared through a hole in the fence. I didn't personally know the people who lived in that house, but I did know one thing about them: they had a large black and white cat.

Standing helplessly in the middle of the road, I thought back to the time when Arthur had shot off in the middle of the jungle. Perhaps it wasn't horses after all that had caught his eye; perhaps it was a jungle cat . . . Whatever it was, Arthur was clearly now on a mission.

'Arthur! Arthur!' I yelled at the top of my voice.

This was not good. I wasn't at all convinced that Arthur would know his way back to the house. He'd only been there twenty-four hours after all and there was a warren of houses and gardens and woods between this house and home.

'Arthur!' I shouted again. Then I decided there was nothing else for it but to go back home and hope that he was either already there or on his way.

But there was no sign of him when I got back.

The TV interviewers were only slightly amused to hear that their star interviewee had done a runner. I tried to reassure them as best I could as Helena and I went out to the back of the house to scour the horizon and the neighbouring gardens for any sign of a big golden dog gone AWOL.

We had both shouted our heads off, when Helena started on her Professional Whistle. This is the most piercing whistle you've ever heard, the kind the people out the front of hotels use to summon a taxi. Except this time there was no sign of a taxi, or an Arthur.

I climbed over our back fence and set off towards the garden that was home to the black and white cat. I had thought that I could hear a distant shout of someone saying 'Hey'. I was so busy looking over towards the cat's garden that I almost missed a rustle in the snowy bushes to my right.

Arthur. He was coming trotting towards me as if nothing in the world were amiss and he hadn't done anything wrong at all. He came up to me and stopped, and then looked up at me as if to say, *What? What's the matter? I just had to investigate something, didn't I?*

I gave him a welcome-back pat because I thought I'd read somewhere that you mustn't punish a dog when he comes back after running off because that would only make him think that coming back means trouble.

Together we walked back towards the house and the television people.

A week later and I reckoned we were beginning to establish a sort of pattern. Arthur seemed to be settling in to his new life in pretty well all the important respects. He mostly did what we wanted him to do, and mostly he 'came' to us when we asked him to. Except if there was a cat in the vicinity.

It was also becoming clear that Arthur's eating habits were a strange mix of survivor and gourmet. You can tell he's a survivor, because when he's had enough, he often takes any food that's left and buries it. On the other hand, Arthur can be quite a picky eater. We ended up giving him a mixture of hard and soft foods – the boring hard bits on top so he'd eat them, with the more interesting bits (beef, liver, chicken) below. But he quickly showed us that his favourite was chicken – thighs, plain and, ideally as it turned out, grilled on the barbecue, just as we cooked them for ourselves.

In fact, he often seemed to be generally quite happy eating what we ate. With one exception: sausages. Who ever heard of a dog who turned up his nose at sausages? Well, we began to realise that we had such a dog.

We only discovered the thing about the sausages when we were trying to train him to sit. We were told that if we held an enticing bit of food above his head and then moved it backwards, he would have to look gradually up and up at it, and eventually therefore sit. When we used a piece of sausage he was quite uninterested in the whole process, but when we tried it with chicken we suddenly had an obedient dog who sat when we asked him to.

He seemed to love the countryside around and – particularly – the snow. Now that it was a bit deeper there seemed to be nothing he liked better than having a good old roll about in it, especially if he'd been on a long run. Extraordinary how he'd adapted to such a different climate; it was almost as if he were meant to be here and not in Ecuador at all.

After a week or so, I decided that it was time to take him shopping. Not just our usual food shopping, but proper dog shopping – going to a special dog store and buying him some welcome-home treats. So after he and I came back from our morning run, I clipped on his short lead, changed my shoes and grabbed my wallet.

Together we walked to the car, and that's when I discovered his inexplicable inability to jump up into the car by himself. Knowing how agile he was, I stood by the open back of the car for a good five minutes, pointing at the empty boot and making jumping signs.

It was suddenly as if Arthur couldn't understand plain Swedish. He just stood stock-still, gazing up at me. He had always jumped into the car if Helena told him to, and if I wasn't around, but at that moment I realised that if I ever wanted Arthur in the car with me I was going to have to lift him.

I thought about this as I drove into town. We'd read a few 'animal behaviourist' books while Arthur was in quarantine, since we had no idea what to expect and no experience of having a dog in the house. So by the time Arthur arrived we felt we knew all about the theories of dogs and their packs, and top dogs, and commands, and eating before the dog does, and not paying too much attention so the dog doesn't feel that it is 'top dog'.

I was pretty sure that one thing you really shouldn't do is succumb to a sort of emotional blackmail within a few days of the dog's arrival. But then rules like that weren't really made for Arthurs.

When we got to the dog shop, I could tell that Arthur was a bit excited. I suppose if you were a dog and you got taken into a place full of the smells of nice dog things – like all kinds of dog food – then you would get excited. Unfortunately, this took the form of Arthur having a pee in the corner of the shop. The owner was not amused.

Knowing who Arthur was – as everyone in the area did – he launched into a small lecture. 'You have to be firm, you know,' he said. 'It's about control. A dog needs to know what the rules are and who's boss.'

I nodded as politely as I could, paid for the Dentastix and food that I'd chosen and led Arthur quickly out of the shop. I had a feeling this wouldn't be the last time someone would tell me how to 'control' Arthur, telling me how to teach him and how to be tough with him. But that wasn't my style. Maybe my style isn't the right way, but I was determined that if Arthur was going to learn things it would be because he wanted to, not because he was threatened.

I wanted him to feel part of the family, I wanted him to feel safe and loved. And I was determined that I should always show him how happy I was to see him, even if I was in a rush. I was sure that was important.

All the books say the one thing you shouldn't do is make dogs human, to treat them like people.

I had a feeling that was exactly what I was going to do.

Chapter 15

A Home Run

'We run for those who can't' – Wings for Life

In the middle of all this there was, of course, the day job. Although 'job' is not how a lot of people would describe it, managing and leading Team Peak Performance keeps me busy, if not 24/7, then pretty much 18/7. When Philippa was born, a lot of people thought I might get a proper job. Some people even offered me one. And maybe if I'd said yes I'd have some idea of where the money's going to come from when I'm sixty-five.

But that's not my way. I have no idea where the money's going to come from when I'm sixty-five; all I think about – apart from my family – is the next race. That's why I'd take standing on the winner's podium over a bag full of two-million-dollar-notes any time. Ideally, standing on the podium with Philippa and Thor in my arms. (There was a time, not so long ago, when I'd see racers stand on the podium with their small child on their arm. I'd hated it. Give me a break, I'd think. Now, of course, it is a very different story . . .)

And anyway, I tell myself, money is only for living off, for doing stuff, not putting in the bank.

I sometimes think that maybe the next race will be my last – I certainly start each race as if it were, putting everything into it. But after nearly twenty years of racing I feel I'm at my peak. Experience has taught me how to prepare mentally as well as physically, and also when to hold back on training – for example, I'd never go for long bike sessions in the rain; I know only too well how easy it is to get sick doing that, and so I take fewer risks now.

Still, making it all happen is labour-intensive work, and we had races and training sessions in Chile and Crete to plan for the first half of the year, and an important World Series race in Swaziland to get ready for in June. But before that we had another race to compete in. And this time Arthur was coming too.

The Wings for Life World Run, held in early May, is in aid of research into spinal cord injury. It's a race for runners and wheelchair racers that starts at exactly the same time in thirty-odd countries all over the world. Half an hour after the race begins, a 'catcher car' drives at particular speeds behind the runners, and when it catches up with them it uses tracking technology to clock each runner off – so the fastest runner is the last to be 'caught'. In the first ever Wings for Life race the first runner was caught in France after five kilometres, the last – and therefore the worldwide winner – in Austria at 79.9 kilometres.

We had decided that this would be a chance for Arthur to be reunited with the team and to have a good day out for a good cause. Also, we thought that people would like to see how well Arthur was getting on and how full of beans he was. Although there were plenty of people offering us money for Arthur to advertise things, we didn't want him to do things like that. This, on the other hand, was for such a good cause and was a nice way for his fans to see Arthur in action.

So we didn't exactly do training with him, but I started to take him on some longer runs to see how he got on.

Our first day of 'training' was about two weeks before the actual race. I was up early and had come thundering downstairs, anxious to get on and out into the bright April morning.

My co-runner didn't seem to sense my urgency at all. As I went into the sitting room, there he was in what I was coming to realise was his absolutely favourite Arthur sleeping position. Flat on his back with his paws in the air and deeply, deeply asleep.

As I looked down at him, I couldn't help thinking how vulnerable he looked. Belly-up and completely unprotected. He must, I thought, be utterly and totally relaxed to sleep so well and so unguardedly. Perhaps that was also why he'd so often make a point of lying in the middle of the floor or the hallway – it means we have to step over him, show him respect. I'm sure he likes knowing we'll do that, that he's safe and we won't kick him or anything. Just as I was thinking this he opened one eye, wriggled himself round into a sitting position and was standing by the front door before I could give him a good-morning pat.

Tongue out, panting slightly with the eager anticipation of a run, he looked up at me with such endearingly wide-awake excitement that his morning hello pat turned into a full-blown cuddle.

I decided that that morning we would give ourselves a good long run and drive to the Golden Trail, on top of the hill overlooking the lakes. It seemed absurd to be lifting him into the car like an old dog when we were off for a good long run, but I knew by now that being lifted up by me was non-negotiable in Arthur-world.

When we arrived and had set off into the crisp morning air, he kept pace with me as expertly as ever. It was great to stretch my legs like this, I thought, with Arthur totally in sync by my side. We'd been going steadily for half an hour or so when I saw someone coming towards us. A walker with two poles was striding up the path.

I felt Arthur get out of sync and start pulling, and then – as the walker got nearer – he started to pull much harder. As the guy came up to us, Arthur started barking and jumping about and seemed to be trying to get away. The walker hadn't made any sudden movements, and in fact looked very disconcerted by the effect he was having on Arthur. But by now Arthur was pretty manic and nearly yanking the lead out of my hand.

'Arthur,' I shouted to him. 'Hey, what's the matter?'

The walker decided to take the path of least resistance, and with a wry look walked past us and quickly climbed the path behind us.

As he receded into the distance Arthur calmed down a bit. And then, once the walker had disappeared, Arthur went back to being his old self. Looking up at me, he seemed to be saying, *OK, let's get back to our run now.*

There must be a history to this, I thought, as we ran on down the hill. After all, I'd seen Arthur unperturbed by so many things. Only the day before, when we were all on a walk, there had been a sudden gunshot from the woods. Helena and Philippa and I had jumped out of our skins, but Arthur seemed quite unfazed.

I supposed we'd never really know what had happened to him, but I had a bad feeling that somewhere along the line a man and a stick had played a part.

Meanwhile, Philippa was getting used to the new member of the family in her own way. We'd noticed that if Arthur came across someone – old or young – who behaved as if they were nervous or frightened of him, he'd give a kind of low-level growl. Perhaps he associated that behaviour with people who might throw stones at him or kick him – after all, that's how a lot of people behave towards 'street dogs' in Ecuador. But if he was with children, or women, he'd be relaxed and gentle. Although he sometimes jumps up at Helena and puts his mouth round her wrist (his classic Just Playing thing to do) he's gentler with her than he is with me.

I knew that to start with, and however gentle Arthur was, Philippa would be a little bit afraid of him. He was, after all, a lot bigger than her. And at the beginning he sensed her nervousness, and went a bit easier on her – that is, he sort of ignored her, and didn't react to her exploratory proddings and pokings. He didn't snap or turn on her like you might expect from a dog who had to be aware of threat all the time. (Although if you rushed at him from behind, quickly and unexpectedly, as a cyclist once did, he would turn round and bark and be prepared to defend himself.)

Perhaps his approach to people was a bit like his approach to other dogs, a sort of mature tolerance but with an extra dose of acceptance for anyone who was associated with me.

One day soon after Arthur had arrived, a neighbour's dog, a small, lively young dog called Ludde, came round to play.

He bounced around and made lots of noise, trying his best to get maximum attention from Arthur. And it was wonderful to see how Arthur, from his Olympian heights of age and experience, seemed to enjoy Ludde's high-spiritedness. Soon they were playing around together – mock-biting each other, chasing each other in circles – like a couple of puppies.

It was particularly great to see because the day before we had been round to visit friends who also had a young dog – a very energetic pitbull. That time the jumping around and biting hadn't been so friendly, and although Arthur did his best to bat off the younger dog, things got very noisy.

Eventually we all decided to shut the pitbull in a different part of the house. Which worked fine until one of their children let him back out. The pitbull went back to barking and baiting Arthur, and Arthur went back to pushing him back down. Not in an aggressive way, but in an 'I'm the boss, now stop it' kind of way.

It was a while before we saw Arthur at all put out by another dog. But I suppose it had to happen some time, and it happened when we were visiting neighbours. This time, the dog was slightly bigger than Arthur, also of indeterminate breed, and a girl dog. Now someone, somehow, at some point along the way in Ecuador (probably one of the dog charities that work there) had operated on Arthur and made sure that there would never be any little Arthurs. Which is a bit sad, really, as Arthur would make a splendid father. But Arthur doesn't know this, so he started to make overtures to the rather bigger girl dog and even got so far as to try to climb up her.

I've never seen Arthur so disconcerted as when the big girl dog pushed him off and gave him a bit of a cuff on the nose.

The Wings for Life race was going to happen in Kalmar on the island of Öland in south-east Sweden. It was a bit of a long journey to get there from Örnsköldsvik, but it was all in a good cause, and besides it was a good way to get together with Staffan and Simon and another member of the Peak Performance team, Marika (who's also a regular part of the team, since Karen is mostly based in the States).

When we got there, it was a spectacular sight. The start of the race was by Kalmar's imposing castle and the square around the castle was heaving with colourful athletes and enthusiastic spectators. The sun was shining brightly, and you could see the race route wending its way out through picturesque open farmland and along the sandy coastline.

Even though she was six months pregnant, Helena was going to run, pushing Philippa in the buggy, and I was going to run with Arthur's lead tied to my belt. We all had our Peak Performance kit on and our backpacks, so we looked more like adventure racers.

The press were out in force and so were Arthur's fans. There were about three thousand athletes, and many thousands more spectators. It was a big moment for Arthur, but nobody had thought to tell him that. As the time came for the race to start, the five of us milled around the front of the first group of racers. I looked down proudly at Arthur.

He was fast asleep.

'Perhaps we should let him get his strength up,' said Helena as she got Philippa into the buggy and ready for the race. 'Be good if you could get to the ten-k mark.'

The object of this race, unlike any other I'd ever been in, wasn't to win, but even though Arthur and I hadn't yet run that far, I thought we could do better than ten k.

We'd been given lots of Arthur's favourite dried beef by the organisers as we waited for the start and talked to the press – perhaps that's what had made him sleepy. But with one minute to go to the starting gun, I thought I'd better wake him up. He was instantly on his feet and raring to go.

The gun roared and – boom! – Arthur was off.

He pulled on ahead as if his only goal was a gold medal. He was running so strongly that he was almost pulling my belt off. It wasn't the time to tell him to conserve his strength for later. Arthur was on a mission. We ran together, with Helena doing a great job of pushing Philippa's buggy just behind us, out of the city and towards the coastline.

The crowds lining the route seemed to be thirty, forty people thick. All we could hear were cries of, 'Go, Arthur!' 'You guys are great!' and 'Hey, Arthur, we love you!'

We ran up to the seven-kilometre mark and that's when Helena decided – quite understandably – that she had had enough. We all paused to get some water – the afternoon sun was pretty high by now, and running was thirsty work.

After that we set off again, buoyed up by the wonderful things the crowd were shouting as we ran past them.

After eleven or twelve kilometres Arthur wasn't pulling at his lead. In fact, he was starting to slow down a lot. But somehow he kept going: the crowd seemed to have an effect on him too, and so did our fellow runners, who slapped us on the back and said 'Great stuff' and 'You guys rock' as they overtook us.

Five kilometres and a water-stop later, and Arthur was now only trotting. Someone in the crowd yelled out very loudly, 'Hey, Arthur! Superstar! We love you!' and it could have been my imagination but I could swear there was a bit more spring in Arthur's step every time someone said something like that.

But we couldn't go on for ever, and at about the eighteen-kilometre mark we called a halt.

We headed off for team photos and some sustaining water and beef for Arthur, and got ready for the journey home. Although Arthur probably wasn't going to make a habit of competitive sport, I could tell as I lifted him into the car that he'd enjoyed his first race for Peak Performance.

Back in Örnsköldsvik and it was time to get into intensive training for the second World Series race of the season – in Swaziland in June. We were going to start with some training in Greece and then head off to what would be a crucial race.

We would be nearly the same team as Team Ecuador – me, Staffan and Karen, but this time with Jonas Andersson instead of Simon. And we would be facing some stiff competition – particularly from the South African teams, who this time were on home ground – as well as some very demandingly hilly country.

So we all needed to be in good shape. I did a kind of inventory on myself and reckoned that my own training was going well despite some of my old injuries flaring up. I have so many bits of me that have been bashed in racing – from both my little fingers, which are permanently bent, to cracked teeth, an injured spine (probably from too many collisions when I played hockey), a dislocated shoulder that still hurts and needs treatment every week, damage to both knees from running (especially the one that was so badly stitched up in Finland) and one foot that's never really been the same after running with no heel and the other after running with black, frostbitten toes for six days. (Once, during Primal Quest USA, I got them to bandage up that foot to keep the toes intact. The explosion when they took the bandages off was not a pretty sight.)

By and large I think I've been incredibly lucky to still be in such good shape after so many incidents. Many of my near-death experiences haven't had witnesses, but I know that two of my team back in 2009 won't forget one of my most dramatic ones in a hurry. I was climbing a difficult mountain above a forest in Brazil. About ten or fifteen metres up I missed a handhold and flew off the side of the mountain. In mid-air I somehow managed to do a full backflip and landed on my feet. Perfect landing, I remember thinking, before I crashed into the bushes and stopped. My teammates were horrified and thought I'd had it. But I stood up ten minutes later and started to climb the cliff face again. We finished the race – and we came third.

We arrived in Swaziland in good spirits, and set off on the first leg of the 500-kilometre race with a complicated strategy of saving ourselves for the crucial canyoneering and caving sections. There was a compulsory dark zone after the first seven legs, which was the beginning of the kayaking section. How we played all this against the other teams and our own exhaustion was, we knew, going to be critical.

The first steep climb was OK, and we were doing well by the time we got to the caving section – crawling and trekking through 800 metres of massive caves. After the dark zone, we felt in great shape for the next leg, which was a cycling leg. We raced really well, were utterly focused and scarcely took time to look at the zebras and crocodiles we passed on the way. We were more interested in the four teams we overtook to reach second place with less than 100 kilometres to go.

But the last leg was incredibly tough. It was cold, dark and difficult to navigate. Just to add to the fun, something went wrong with my insides and I couldn't keep down any food. By the time we were on the last trekking stage we knew there were at least two teams right on our heels.

Heads down and determined, we made it to the finish – a great team effort. Only an hour ahead of the next team, but good enough to get the bronze.

It was a pretty happy result. A bronze medal. And soon I'd be home with Helena, Philippa . . . and Arthur.

As I got on the plane to go back to Örnsköldsvik I was glad it was a good long flight. It gave me plenty of time to dwell on the fact that one way and another life was pretty good.

There wasn't much time for dwelling when I got back. 'Our' race, the July SwimRun at the Höga Kusten (High Coast), was only a month away and, as race organisers, we needed to make sure every step and stroke of the race was thought through. This meant Staffan and me planning the course, and going over it a number of times to make sure that it was all do-able – if difficult.

The SwimRun is a race of teams of two who run through forests and rocky trails on the High Coast Islands – and swim the bits in between. The race is nearly forty kilometres long and involves getting in and out of the water around thirty times. Like any kind of adventure racing, it involves great technique and great stamina.

This was our first year setting up the race and we really wanted it to become an annual feature on the SwimRun calendar. The pressure was on to get it right.

Staffan and I set off soon after we were back from Swaziland to finalise the whole scoping process. And of course the newest member of the team came with us.

When we arrived at the jumping-off point for the race – Gullviks Havsbad, a village on one of the sandy beaches south-east of Örnsköldsvik – Arthur, Staffan and I had a lot of work to do.

It was a bright sunny day, and hot going, but there was a great deal of ground to cover and no time to sit about and admire the view.

We took a boat out to the first of the islands and started checking out the rocky trail through the middle of it. Lots of the paths were super-steep, but Arthur seemed pretty relaxed, even though this was all strange new country to him. Even when he was at the top of a particularly difficult climb, with not much in the way of clues as to where the path led, he was usually out in front, keen to check out the new smells and trotting confidently ahead, knowing, I guess, that we were close behind and he was safe.

For parts of the race we couldn't take the boat, and anyway we needed to scope out the swims by actually doing them. We started the first swim after a couple of hours. It began with a jump off one of the rocky islands and ended at the water's edge on the next island about two hundred metres away.

I jumped in first and looked behind me to see what Arthur was making of it all. This was his first serious swim, after all, since those dramatic struggles in Ecuador, and I still wasn't really sure how comfortable he was in the water for long stretches. But there was no need to worry; Arthur jumped straight in after me, unhesitatingly and confidently. Staffan followed behind.

For the first part of the stretch I swam side by side with Arthur, who was splashing forwards enthusiastically as if to say, *I can do this, watch me!* Glad that he seemed to be getting the hang of it so well, I ploughed on ahead. After about sixty metres I realised I couldn't hear Arthur splashing. I looked back.

Arthur had slowed down completely, and was looking uncertain as he doggy-paddled towards me. I could tell that he'd changed his mind. He didn't like this long-distance swimming thing after all.

I waited for him to catch up. He came towards me, and then, just as I was about to turn round and carry on, he made a beeline for me and before I knew it had jumped up on my back.

He was wriggling and scrambling about, and I could feel my wetsuit getting cut to ribbons by his claws, but by that stage it was all I could do to concentrate on not sinking. With thirty kilos plus of wet, wriggly dog on top of you, it is very difficult to keep afloat.

With about fifty metres to go, I seriously wondered if we weren't just going to go under and stay there. I turned to Staffan, calling, 'Hey, help me here.' But as I turned I realised I was talking to myself. Staffan had swum on ahead to get his camera. Great, I thought. At least our last moments will be photographed for posterity.

But somehow we made it to the other side of the lake and, despite feeling a little bruised by the whole experience, we had enough energy to finish scoping out the race.

The day of the race itself also happened to be the day of a huge freak summer storm. There were big waves when there ought to have been no waves, and it was altogether lucky that none of the teams got washed out to sea.

Still, it was generally deemed to be a great success, and I'm sure – at least I hope I'm sure – that the Höga Kusten SwimRun is an annual fixture here to stay.

By the time the summer proper had started, it was clear that – while not wanting to risk another long and arduous swim – Arthur was a bit of a water-dog. Whenever we went for a long and hot run, he had an amazing ability to sniff out a good deep puddle or the nearest lake for a cooling splash.

We decided he was generally behaving a lot like a normal Swedish family dog. A bit puppy-like sometimes, and a bit disobedient at others. In fact, despite the 'sit' training, there was really only one instruction you could absolutely rely on him to obey. It involved having your running shoes on and standing by the front door; you simply had to say, 'Let's go' and you could be sure that Arthur would be up and after you almost instantly.

Just as the weather was starting to get hotter, and being nine months pregnant was starting to get rather uncomfortable, Helena started to feel the pains that could only mean one thing. She was rushed to hospital and, on 18 August 2015, Thor was born.

Thor is, without doubt, the most perfect little baby boy ever to have been born. He immediately took to life in the Lindnord family and quickly got the hang of eating, sleeping and not crying except when he had something to say.

We had talked to Philippa a lot about how she was going to have a little baby brother. We wanted her to get used to the idea in just the same way as we had wanted her to get used to the idea of Arthur. And although she was a little disconcerted by Thor's arrival for the first few days, she quickly got used to the idea that here was a new playmate and someone for us all to love.

I felt sure that the tolerance and love of parents have an enormous effect on children, and that it is an intrinsic part of bringing them up. As the Pippi Longstocking author Astrid Lindgren said, 'If you give your children love, love and more love, the common sense will come by itself.' Helena and I never shout at each other, we never scream or yell, nor are we intolerant or angry at other people. Anger and hate don't make for anything good, but an atmosphere of love and calm breeds contentment.

But it was all very well having a plan for Philippa and Thor. What about Arthur, people kept asking? How will he react to a new person in the household, a new person to take my attention? Everyone pointed out – indeed, it was impossible not to see – that Arthur's world revolved around me. There was an extraordinary connection between us that never ceased to astonish me and make me happy. I was certain that the combination of Arthur's natural gentleness and the fact that Thor was clearly so important to me would make him as gentle with him as he was with Philippa.

The test came very quickly. We had only been back at home about an hour and were sitting on the sofa admiring our new son when Anders, Helena's father, came back to the house. He had just taken Arthur for a long walk, and came through the door still holding Arthur on the lead.

I was sitting on the sofa, behind the coffee table, with Thor on my knee. As soon as Arthur came into the room he seemed to be on a mission. Like an Exocet missile he yanked the lead out of Anders' hand and pushed himself roughly through Anders' legs. Jumping up and over the table, he made a beeline for the sofa right next to my lap.

Everyone reacted in horror, reaching out to try to keep Arthur back.

'No, no,' I said, 'don't worry, it's fine,' hoping against hope that all my instincts about Arthur were right. And then as soon as Arthur was near enough, he gave Thor a tiny nudge with his nose, quickly gave him two little licks on the top of his head, jumped down and went to have a drink from his water bowl.

Helena's parents looked rather taken aback, but Helena and I just smiled at each other.

It couldn't have been clearer: Arthur was welcoming Thor to our family.

And so now it is a year later. A most extraordinary year.

Where we were three we are now five.

And where I never had the remotest idea or intention of having a dog, I now have a friend whose loyalty and devotion I know I can count on to our dying day. Just as I'm sure Arthur knows he can count on mine.

There will never be enough time to dwell on how lucky I am, but I know I will never forget to be thankful that our adventure has had the happiest of endings.

Epilogue:

The Arthur Foundation

'It's not OK to kick them . . .'

Until the race in Ecuador, the only things I knew about stray dogs in other countries were that they were probably diseased and possibly even rabid, and that if they came towards you to attack you, the way to fend them off was to wait until absolutely the last moment, when they were nearly upon you, and then squirt them on the nose with water. (They have to be really close, so you have to really hold your nerve. But adventure racers always have a water bottle handy and, usually, some nerve.)

But what I didn't know, until my experience with Arthur, is quite what a doomed and terrible life these dogs mostly lead. In some parts of South American countries there is very little respect for animals, and no tradition of looking after them – of having them as pets, living in the house and being 'owned'.

In rural areas of Ecuador there are some dogs, known as '*callejizados*', who started out belonging to someone but who end up roaming free and eating what they can find by scavenging. But most strays, or street dogs, particularly in towns, are just left to their own devices and are frequently ill-treated by the local people. They roam the streets in huge numbers: in Quito alone there are over 170,000 street dogs, surviving on trash and occasional charity.

It struck me then, and it seems from talking to Ismael and all the other good people who try to help, that it has just never been part of the culture for some parts of Ecuador to regard animals with any respect. They are kicked, shouted at, beaten – people know that there are no laws to protect the rights of animals, and it is not a crime to mistreat them, so people mistreat animals and they let their children mistreat them.

Well, it is not OK to kick dogs. It is not OK to beat them and let them starve.

There are two ways in which we would like our foundation to help the Arthurs of this world.

The first is to adopt them and show them love and a loving family – possible, of course, for only the tiniest fraction of street dogs. But if as many animals as possible can be rounded up and looked after in rescue centres – in the hope that, perhaps at some point, someone might come and take them in to look after them permanently – that would help.

And the second way is for governments – central and local – to make it a crime to mistreat animals.

At the moment there is no such law, and that is what the people who support the immediate adoption of the Law on Animal Welfare (or LOBA to give it its Spanish acronym) are trying to change. They want a mass implementation of a law that protects animals – as well as sterilisation campaigns, and campaigns for mass adoptions.

This is what I would like our foundation to help with; to try to make a change to the long-term condition of strays, and to help in the short term with rescues and adoptions.

Acknowledgements

I am not a hero. I am just an ordinary guy who followed his heart in an extraordinary situation. Arthur and I would never have had a happy ending if it hadn't been for the support of so many people.

I thank them all, particularly:

Krister Göransson, talented photographer and good friend without whose photographs this story would never have captured the headlines; **Staffan Björklund, Simon Niemi, Karen Lundgren,** my friends and teammates who also fought to make the miracle happen; our support team **Malin Andersson, Sara Olsson, Mia Renz** and, of course, **Helena Lindnord,** who worked so hard for us day and night; **Peak Performance** and everyone who supported the Arthur Foundation; the wonderful **Debbie Dunagan** and all at ScandiPet; everyone at Anicura especially **Johan Hamilton**; the miracle-worker **Ismael Carrión** and all who helped in Ecuador; the great **Lena Bergman** who helped us manage the press.

And thank you:

Robert Åström, for being a great friend and helping hand with Arthur when we are away: Arthur loves his adventures with you.

Val Hudson, the writer whose understanding of our story, and whose ability to understand me and Arthur so well, is matched only by your fantastic way with words. I have enjoyed our long conversations; talking to you is like talking to a best friend.

My father, who started me on the road to sport when I was six years old, and will always be my companion in life; you have my support whatever happens.

My mother, for all the support.

Philippa, you are Dad's princess and I love everything about you. You are still very young but you never say no to a new adventure and to trying new things.

Thor, we named you after a heroic god, because we think the name suits you. You are just a little boy as this book is published, but when you read it you will be much older and wiser.

Above all, my thanks go to you, **Helena,** for your belief in me and all my adventures. You have a golden heart, and can never say a bad word about anyone, ever. I still remember the first time I saw you, just if it were yesterday. You are my east, west, north and south.

And finally, my thanks to **Arthur.** For being Arthur. And for finding me.

Picture Acknowledgements

© Michael Bergman: Colour image in plate section, number 21
© Krister Göransson: Integrated pictures on pages 3, 47, 57, 68, 69, 86, 88, 108, 116, 125, 133, 140, 141, 154, 157, 171, 175, 176, 190, 194, 202, 269
Colour images in plate sections, numbers 3, 4, 5, 6, 7, 8, 9, 10, 11, 12, 13, 14, 15, 16, 17, 18, 19, 20, 22, 23, 24, 25, 26, 27, 28, 29
© Kate Hewson: Maps p vi–vii
© Val Hudson: Integrated pictures on pages 1, 33, 215, 230
© Jens Kristofferson: Integrated picture on page 242.
Colour image in plate section, number 34
© Helena and Mikael Lindnord: Integrated pictures on pages 16, 18, 31, 49, 52, 220, 222, 233, 240, 248, 254, 264, 265, 268
Colour images in plate sections, numbers 1, 2, 30, 31, 32, 33, 35, 36, 38
© Håkan Nordström: Colour image in plate section, number 37
© Richard Ström: integrated picture on page 257

275

Mikael Lindnord is an adventure racer and race planner. As a boy he wanted to be an ice hockey player, but failing to make a professional team at the age of 17 set him on a different path. after doing military service he became an adventure racer. He has been travelling the world and racing in the AR World Series ever since. When not racing he lives with his wife, children and, of course, his dog Arthur.

Arthur is a mongrel from somewhere in Ecuador. He likes meatballs, long runs with Mikael and relaxing with his family in Sweden.

As an editor of non-fiction at major publishing houses, **Val Hudson** published many ground-breaking bestsellers. Now a full-time writer, she is the author of a wide range of non-fiction and, as Chloe Bennet, the 'BoyWatching' series of novels for young teens.

stories ... voices ... places ... lives

We hope you enjoyed *Arthur*. If you'd like to know more
about this book or any other title on our list,
please go to www.tworoadsbooks.com

For news on forthcoming Two Roads titles, please sign
up for our newsletter

enquiries@tworoadsbooks.com

TwoRoadsBooks